Sonia Allison

KINGSWOOD COOKBOOKS

SELECTED MICROWAVE RECIPES

SERIES EDITOR JUDY RIDGWAY

Photography
SUE ATKINSON
Mike Roles Studio

The Kingswood Press

Text copyright © by Sonia Allison
Photographs copyright © 1985 by Sue Atkinson, Mike Roles Studio
Published in Great Britain by
The Kingswood Press
(an imprint of William Heinemann Ltd)
Kingswood, Tadworth, Surrey
All rights reserved
Reproduced and proofed by Imago Publishing Ltd
Printed and bound in Great Britain by
W.S. Cowell Ltd, Ipswich
0 434 98070 6

CONTENTS

LIST OF ILLUSTRATIONS

ACKNOWLEDGEMENTS AND THANKS TO:

Home economist
Pamela Gwyther

Loan of Tableware
The Reject Shop, Knightsbridge

MICROWAVE HINTS

USE AND CARE OF THE MICROWAVE OVEN

1. *Look after your oven*
Cleaning it immediately after use will keep it spotless and fresh; regular servicing by a qualified engineer will ensure it functions efficiently. To clean the interior of the microwave easily, dampen a dish cloth and heat for 30 to 45 seconds at defrost setting. Wipe over top, base and sides of oven then dry with a clean tea towel. Do this frequently to prevent food spills from sticking to the inside. Alternatively, and to freshen the oven at the same time, put about ½ pt/275 ml bowl of cold water inside the oven. Add a slice or two of fresh lemon or lime. Heat at full power for 3 minutes or until boiling fast and oven steams up. Wipe interior clean with a dish cloth then dry with a tea towel.

2. Never preheat a microwave oven or operate when empty. Without food or drink to absorb the microwaves they will bounce straight back to the magnetron, or microwave energy generator, and damage it. Similarly, melting half teaspoons of fat or heating tiny amounts of liquid will have the same effect, so place a tumbler of water in the oven at the same time. To prevent an empty oven being switched on by accident, keep a container of water inside until the oven is needed for cooking.

3. *Power Controls*

All recipes in this book have been prepared in a 600 watt output oven, using only two power settings: COOK/HIGH – 100% power (600 watts) and DEFROST – 50% (300 watts). If your oven has a different output, the guide below may prove useful.

For a 500 watt output oven, *increase* cooking time by about one-fifth (20%). e.g. 10 minutes becomes 12 minutes.

For a 550 watt output oven, *increase* cooking time by about one-tenth (10%). e.g. 10 minutes becomes 11 minutes.

For a 650 watt output oven, *decrease* cooking time by one-tenth (10%). e.g. 10 minutes becomes 9 minutes.

For a 700 watt output oven, *decrease* cooking time by about one-fifth (20%). e.g. 10 minutes becomes 8 minutes.

Using these figures will give a fairly accurate conversion time but for greater accuracy refer to your own microwave oven recipe book.

Variable power settings ranging from 1 to 10 are to be found in some models:

Setting 1 equates to 10% of power output and is also termed warm. It is used to keep cooked dishes warm or take the chill off cold ones. It is called either warm or low.

Setting 2 equates to 20% of power output and is recommended for warming or very gentle simmering. It is called either warm or low as well.

Setting 3 equates to 30% of power output and is used for slow defrosting and simmering. It is called either defrost, low, simmer or soften.

Setting 4 equates to 40% of power output and is often chosen for defrosting, braising and stewing. It is called either slow cook, medium, low defrost, stew, simmer or braise.

Setting 5 equates to 50% of power output and is the one used most frequently for defrosting. It can also be used for simmering and stewing. It is called either medium, defrost, simmer or stew.

Setting 6 equates to 60% of power output and is used chiefly for reheating cooked dishes, baking or simmering. It is called either reheat, bake or simmer.

Setting 7 equates to 70% of power output and is used primarily for roasting. It is called either medium high, bake or roast.

Setting 8 equates to 80% of power output and is also used for reheating and baking. It is called either reheat or bake.

Setting 9 equates to 90% of power output and is used for fast cooking of vegetables in fat (i.e. when making a stew). It is called either medium high, roast, fast reheat or sometimes sauté.

Setting 10 equates to 100% of power output and is used for the majority of recipes in this microwave book. It is called either full power, high, maximum or fast cook.

If you have such an oven, follow the instructions for use in your own microwave guide book. Do not try to convert my recipes which were cooked at full power or defrost setting.

4. *Standard recipes are not convertible to microwave ovens so please use only those which have been specifically designed for the appliance – as those in my book.*

Utensils

5. As microwaves only penetrate 1 inch in all directions, choose round and shallow dishes, except when headroom is needed, as for cakes. Oval shaped is second best. Oblong or square dishes can cause uneven cooking, especially at the corners.

6. Never use metal containers or tins as metal reflects microwaves away from the food and prevents it from cooking. The only exceptions are small amounts of tin foil, used to cover poultry wing tips etc to prevent scorching, and metal skewers for kebabs. However, *ensure* that the skewers do not come into contact with any part of the oven interior and are well covered by the surrounding food.

It is also important to note that crockery with manufacturers' names or pattern design printed in gold or silver could cause arcing, which resembles tiny flashes of lightning. This ruins the metallic decoration and also harms the magnetron.

7. In order for the microwaves to reach the food the dishes chosen should be made of material through which the microwaves can pass most readily. These are listed below. Although most stay cool and even cold, some kinds absorb heat from the cooked food and should be removed from the oven with oven gloves.

Baskets These may be used for brief reheating

of rolls etc. Prolonged spells in the microwave cause dryness.

Cling film (See-through plastic wrap) Excellent for covering and lining dishes. To prevent the film from ballooning up in the oven and bursting, or being sucked back on to the food (the latter a disaster if this happens to a pudding which is supposed to rise), I have recommended puncturing the film twice with the tip of a knife to allow steam to escape. By puncturing, I mean a small slit and not a tiny pin-prick.

Glass Not your best crystal but Pyrex type glassware is ideal. Corningware, which is ceramic glass, is also excellent. Other, sturdy, glass may also be used.

Paper Kitchen paper or serviettes may be used to line the oven base if food is to be cooked directly on it (it is a great absorber), and also to cover food to prevent spluttering.

Plastic Use rigid plastic only to prevent collapse, and not empty yogurt or cottage cheese containers! Look for special microwave utensils made by Thorpac, Lakeland Plastics or Anchor Hocking. Just 3 examples though there are more makes stocked by microwave centres, some kitchen boutiques and department stores. Note that plastic spatulas are useful in that they can be left, say, in a sauce while it is cooking and then used for stirring as and when required.

Pottery and porcelain Both may be used but not a best tea or dinner set. Avoid dark utensils as they become very hot.

Roasting bags (Also called Boiling Bags) With a hundred and one uses, see-through plastic roasting bags are convenient to use and also clean. Ideal for cooking joints of meat or poultry, close the tops with elastic bands or string, not metal ties.

Waxed paper products Rather like basketware, these should be used very briefly or the wax will begin to melt.

Wood Wood, like basketware, dries out in the microwave and should be used only for brief reheating.

8. *Browning Dish*
This is a white ceramic dish, the base of which is coated with a special tin oxide material. It becomes very hot indeed when preheated, making it possible to sear food prior to cooking in the microwave. This gives the food a brown finish associated with conventional grilling or frying. As the dish needs to be preheated, empty, for varying lengths of time (depending on the food being cooked), be guided by your own microwave oven instruction book. As a

general rule, the preheating time should be around 6 minutes for steaks and chops and 2 to 3 minutes for eggs. It should never be preheated for longer than 8 minutes, nor used in a conventional oven. The larger the dish, the longer the preheating time required. Thus 5 minutes in a small dish will equate to 7 minutes in a large one. Every time a batch of food has been cooked, the browning dish will need cleaning, greasing and reheating but for half the length of time allowed initially. Although it will take on a yellowy tinge when hot, the dish will return to its original colour when cool. Preheating this type of dish does not harm the oven.

Browning dishes are usually optional extras, to be purchased separately from the oven.

9. *Temperature probe*

This looks like a thick knitting needle attached to a plastic-coated lead and is generally available with the more sophisticated models of microwave ovens. One end slots into the side of the oven while the other end (the needle part) is inserted into the food to be cooked and registers the internal temperature.

The cooking cycle is therefore geared to temperature and not time and when, for example, a joint of well-done beef registers 160°F (71°C), the oven will switch off automatically. As every make of cooker varies, please refer to your own microwave book before using the probe and setting the temperature. The temperature given above is just one example. Pork requires a higher internal temperature; rare beef a lower one.

10. *Thermometers*

Thermometers for use in microwaves are now obtainable and they, too, must be used according to the manufacturers' instructions.

COOKING BY MICROWAVE

11. Where the letter (F) appears by the recipe within this book, this indicates this dish is suitable for freezing.

12. Never pile food up. Place thick pieces towards the outer edge of the dish.

13. Stirring helps to distribute the heat evenly. Where possible similar shaped foods, eg potatoes, should be arranged on a plate or dish in the shape of a hollow triangle, square or ring.

14. In order for heat to penetrate the food and work its way gently from the outside to the centre, take note of the resting or standing times between or after cooking, especially

important with large, dense quantities.

15. It is advisable to undercook a dish and return it briefly to the oven if necessary rather than to add extra time for good measure.

16. Salt and seasonings tend to toughen microwave meat, poultry and offal, so add them halfway through the cooking cycle or at the end.

17. To prevent a face full of steam, tilt the dish or bowl *away* from yourself when uncovering and removing either the lid, plate or cling film.

18. To improvise on a ring mould, cover the outside of a tumbler (straight-sided and smooth) with cling film. Stand in the middle of a round, soufflé-type dish with open end of tumbler facing upwards.

19. *Meat and Poultry*

Most meat and poultry respond well to microwave cooking but, where possible, prime cuts should be chosen as they tenderize more readily than the less expensive and muscular parts of the animal traditionally recommended for braises, stews and hot-pots.

20. All meat should be cut into smaller than usual pieces, such as $\frac{1}{2}$ inch or 1.25 cm cubes instead of larger ones suggested for braising or stewing.

21. It is advisable to 'dry' cook meat or poultry, and sometimes vegetables, for a given length of time before liquid is added as this technique helps to soften the meat.

22. *Shape of Joint*

The more regular the shape the better and more evenly it will cook. As this is not always a viable proposition, wrap the narrow end of the joint (the bony part of a leg of lamb for example) with foil during the first half of cooking time to prevent frizzle and overcooking.

The foil will have no detrimental effect on the workings of the oven, in that there will be much more meat in proportion to foil. If choice is possible, settle for the fillet end of pork or lamb, and a boned and rolled piece of beef or veal.

23. *Tips on Roasting*

A. Roasting Bags These are perfect for microwaved lamb, beef and veal and seem to encourage browning. Simply season and/or baste the joint, slide into a roasting bag and close the top by tying with an elastic band or a piece of string. Cook and stand.

B. If not using a roasting bag, stand the joint in a dish, cover with film and puncture twice with the tip of a knife. If the cooking time recommended is 15 minutes or over per lb/450 g at full power, the joint will brown of its own accord and will not require brushing with baste prior to cooking.

C. For very fatty joints, stand a plastic trivet or 2 inverted saucers into a dish and place meat on top. Cover as directed under point B.

D. When joints have fat on one side only, place into a bag or dish with the fat side down. Turn over half way through cooking.

E. For crisp crackling on pork, rub salad oil and salt well into the scored rind. 'Open' roast by standing in a dish and covering closely with paper to prevent spluttering and soiling the oven interior with splashes of grease. Do not turn at half time but keep crackling-side uppermost all the time.

F. For a golden brown effect, a chicken or turkey should be brushed with baste prior to cooking. If the bird is of the self-basting variety a light brush of soy sauce or sprinkling of paprika is all that is necessary.

G. It is advisable to stuff the crop end only of poultry and leave the body cavity empty. If liked, prepared stuffings may be heated up separately in a greased dish. Times will vary from 3 to 6 minutes at full power, depending on whether the mixture is hot, warm or cold or taken from the refrigerator. And obviously quantity *also* determines the length of time.

H. Wing tips and ends of legs of poultry should be foil-wrapped to prevent overcooking.

I. Birds over 12 lb/5½–6 kg should be roasted conventionally unless the capacity of the microwave is very large.

24. Defrosting Hints

A. To prevent slight cooking on the outside, large joints or birds are best left to defrost naturally, either overnight in a refrigerator or for several hours in the kitchen. This applies particularly to quantities over 12 lb/5½–6 kg.

B. As soon as chops, steaks and poultry joints have defrosted enough to be movable, arrange in a single layer on a plate or in a dish. Never heap up and, for maximum efficiency, arrange in a ring round the edge of the plate or dish.

C. Cover any piece of meat or poultry with cling film or kitchen paper as this speeds up defrosting and helps to keep in the moisture. If preferred, put meat or bird into a roasting bag for defrosting.

25. Cakes

Cake mixture (not fatless sponges) should be made wetter than usual to prevent dryness, and, for the same reason, some cakes should be covered with cling film. Take note of standing times. As the cake cooks the heat spreads through to the centre, and after 15 minutes or so it should be completely cooked. Even after being turned out, seemingly cooked, the base may be runny. All that is then necessary is to return the cake, on its plate, to the microwave for a brief spell of cooking, again checking about 4 times every minute. The thing to avoid is overcooking, otherwise the cake will dry out, harden and in some cases become inedible.

26. Rice and Pasta

Rice should be covered while cooking; pasta on its own should be uncovered unless the recipe states otherwise.

27. Vegetables

Leave firm vegetables to stand 2–3 minutes after cooking, but soft vegetables, e.g. sliced cabbage, tomato halves, mushrooms, may be served straight away.

To avoid scalds take care when dealing with bags of vegetables. Always put the bag into a dish for cooking and lift out with your hand protected by an oven glove. With the top of the bag pointing downwards into the sink, carefully remove the elastic band and gently tip vegetables out into a colander to drain.

28. Eggs

The yolks of eggs destined for poaching, frying or baking should be punctured twice, gently, with the tip of a knife or skewer to break the fine skin or membrane enveloping each. This will subsequently stop the yolks from bursting, spluttering and making a mess all over the oven.

Miscellaneous Foods

29. To prevent chicken livers from popping, pierce each piece with the tip of a knife.

30. To refresh dinner rolls, place in a serviette-lined basket and warm through until the surfaces feel very slightly warm; about 1 to 3 minutes (depending on quantity) at defrost setting.

31. To soften legumes (dried peas and beans etc) and eliminate soaking overnight, wash 8 oz (225 g) of the dried vegetables under cold, running water. Put into dish and add 2 pints (1.25 litres) boiling water. Cover dish with cling film, then puncture twice with the tip of a knife. Cook 4 minutes at full power. Leave to stand 2 hours. Drain and use as required.

32. To soften 14 oz (397 g) of frozen pastry, warm for 2 minutes at defrost setting. Stand 5 to 10 minutes or until pastry is soft enough to roll out.

33. To achieve best results when reheating soups, do so on full power for clear soups and at defrost setting for thick or creamy soups.

34. To rehydrate dried fruits, such as apple rings or prunes, without soaking overnight, put about 8 oz (225 g) into a glass bowl. Cover with boiling water (only just) and cook for $5\frac{1}{2}$ to 8 minutes at full power. Leave to stand 10 minutes, covered, then drain and use as desired.

35. To plump up raisins, currants or sultanas, treat as dried fruits above but reduce cooking time to about 4 to 6 minutes at full power. Stand 5 minutes. Drain and dry.

36. To release and extract more juice from citrus fruits and pomegranates, warm for 15 to 30 seconds (depending on size) at full power. Stand 5 minutes.

37. To soften 8 oz (225 g) brown sugar that has become lumpy, put into a dish with half a slice of very fresh bread. Cover and warm $1\frac{1}{2}$ minutes at defrost setting. Alternatively, heat sugar with a wedge of cut fruit (pear or apple) instead of bread. Another method is to cover sugar with a piece of wet kitchen paper and use neither bread nor fruit.

38. To soften ice cream and loosen jellies (provided they are not in metal tins or moulds), heat 45 seconds at defrost setting. Stand 2 to 3 minutes.

39. To melt golden or other syrups and honey which have become grainy (crystallized), take metal caps off jars and warm, individually, for about 3 minutes at defrost setting.

TOMATO SOUP WITH AVOCADO MAYONNAISE

2 medium, ripe avocados
1 tablespoon lemon juice
1 garlic clove, peeled and sliced (optional)
4 tablespoons mayonnaise
½–1 level teaspoon salt

SOUP
2 cans condensed cream of tomato soup
1 pt/575 ml warm water
12 oz/350 g blanched and skinned tomatoes, cut into strips
seasoning to taste

serves 8

1. Make the Avocado Mayonnaise first and leave aside temporarily while preparing the soup: scoop avocado flesh into food processor bowl or blender goblet.
2. Add lemon juice, garlic, mayonnaise and salt. Run machine until smooth. Spoon out into a dish.
3. Tip both cans of soup into a 4 pt/2.25 litre dish. Mix in water and tomatoes.
4. Cover with a plate and cook 8–10 mins at full power or until soup is hot but not boiling. Stir 4 times.
5. Adjust seasoning to taste then ladle into warm soup bowls or plates. Add a tablespoon of the avocado mixture to each and serve straight away.

BELGIAN LETTUCE SOUP

2 oz/50 g butter or margarine
6 oz/175 g onions, peeled and grated
8 oz/225 g green lettuce (round variety), washed well then rinsed and shredded
1 pt/575 mls single cream
2 level tablespoons cornflour
½ pt/275 ml boiling water or chicken stock
1 to 2 level teaspoons salt
butter for garnish

serves 6

1. Put butter or margarine into a 3 pt/1.75 litre deepish casserole dish. Melt 1½–2 mins at defrost setting.
2. Mix in onions and lettuce. Cover with plate or matching lid and cook 3 minutes at full power.
3. Transfer to blender goblet with one third of the cream. Run machine until ingredients are mixed to a purée.
4. Return to dish. Mix in cornflour, remaining cream, boiling water or stock and the salt.
5. Cover as before then cook soup for 15 mins at full power, whisking gently at the end of every 3 mins.
6. Add 1 teaspoon butter to each portion before serving.

AVOCADO SOUP WITH BEETROOT

1½ pt (just under 1 litre) hot chicken stock
2 medium sized and ripe avocados
1 tablespoon lemon juice
1 level teaspoon onion powder
½ to 1 level teaspoon salt
3 oz/75 g grated cooked beetroot

serves 6

1. Pour chicken stock into a bowl and cover with a plate. Heat for 4½ mins at full power.
2. Meanwhile halve avocados, remove flesh and mash *very finely* with lemon juice and onion powder. Alternatively, work to a purée in a blender or food processor.
3. Whisk into soup with salt. Cover as above. Reheat for 3 mins at full power, turning bowl twice unless oven has a turntable.
4. Ladle into warm bowls or plates, garnish each serving with 2 teaspoons grated beetroot, and serve straight away.

TIP *Do not reheat leftovers as flavour and colour will spoil*

CURRY RICE SOUP

2 oz/50 g butter or margarine

4 oz/125 g onions, peeled and chopped or grated

6 oz/175 g well-scrubbed celery, cut into thin
  strips

1 level tablespoon curry powder

2 tablespoons medium sherry

$1\frac{3}{4}$ pt/1 litre chicken stock (use cubes and water
  in the absence of the real thing)

4 oz/125 g easy-cook, long grain rice

1 level teaspoon salt

1 tablespoon soy sauce

6 oz/175 g cooked cold chicken, cut into strips

thick yogurt or soured cream for serving

serves 6 (F)

1. Put butter or margarine in a 4 pt/2.25
litre dish and melt, uncovered, $1\frac{1}{2}$–2 mins at
defrost setting.
2. Add onions and celery. Leave uncovered
and cook 5 mins at full power, stirring once.
3. Mix in curry powder, sherry, stock, rice,
salt and soy sauce. Cover with a plate and
cook 10 mins at full power, stirring twice.
4. Add chicken and continue to cook a
further 5 mins at full power. Stir round, ladle
into soup plates or bowls and top each with
1 tablespoon of yogurt or soured cream.

RUSTIC TOMATO SOUP

*Serve with crusty brown bread or rolls spread with either
butter or peanut butter.*

Illustrated on page 17

2 lb/900 g blanched tomatoes, skinned and
  quartered

2 oz/50 g butter or margarine

4 oz/125 g celery, scrubbed and finely chopped

4 oz/125 g onions, peeled and finely chopped

4 rounded teaspoons dark brown soft sugar

$1\frac{1}{2}$ level teaspoons salt

$\frac{1}{2}$ pt/275 ml hot water

2 level tablespoons cornflour

8 tablespoons cold water

serves 6 to 8 (F)

1. Blend tomatoes to a purée in a blender or
food processor. Leave aside temporarily.
2. Put butter or margarine into a 3 pt/1.75
litre glass or pottery dish and heat 1 min at
full power.
3. Mix in celery and onions. Cover dish with
plate or lid and cook 3 mins at full power.
4. Add sugar, salt, hot water and the tomato
purée (made under point one). Cover as
above or use cling film, puncturing twice
with the tip of a knife. Cook 8 mins at
fullpower, turning dish 4 times unless oven
has a turntable.
5. Uncover. Blend in cornflour, mixed
smoothly with water.
6. Leave uncovered and cook a further 8
mins at full power, stirring 4 times. Ladle
into bowls and serve while still very hot.

OMELETTE AUX FINES HERBS

melted butter or margarine

3 eggs (size 2 or 3)

$\frac{1}{4}$ level teaspoon salt

2 tablespoons cold water

pepper to taste

1 heaped tablespoon finely chopped, mixed fresh
  herbs, e.g. parsley, chives and basil

serves 1 to 2

1. Brush a fairly shallow, 8 in/20 cm round
glass or pottery dish with melted butter or
margarine.
3. Beat eggs *very thoroughly* with all
remaining ingredients except herbs –
breaking them up lightly, as for traditional
omelets, is not enough.
3. Pour into dish and put into microwave.
Cover with plate. Cook $1\frac{1}{2}$ mins at full
power. Turn dish half round unless oven has
a turntable. Shower omelet mixture with
herbs.
4. Uncover then stir egg mixture gently with
a wooden spoon or fork, bringing the
partially set edges to the centre. Return to
microwave and cover as before. Cook
another $1\frac{1}{2}$ mins at full power.
5. Uncover and cook $\frac{1}{2}$–1 min or until top is
just set. Fold into 3 like an envelope and
carefully slide out on to a warm plate. Serve
straight away.

MINESTRONE

12 oz/350 g topped and tailed courgettes,
unpeeled and thinly sliced

8 oz/225 g carrots, peeled and thinly sliced

8 oz/225 g onions, peeled and coarsely chopped

4 oz/125 g green cabbage, washed and shredded

4 oz/125 g white cabbage, washed and shredded

2 oz/50 g celery, scrubbed and very thinly sliced

6 oz/175 g potatoes, peeled and diced

4 oz/125 g fresh or frozen sliced green beans

4 oz/125 g fresh or frozen peas

1 can (14 oz/400 g) tomatoes

2 rounded tablespoons tomato purée

2 oz/50 g small pasta or long grain rice

1¾ pt/1 litre boiling water

3 to 4 level teaspoons salt

serves 8 to 10 (F)

1. Put all the fresh and frozen vegetables into a 6 pt (about 3.5 litre) bowl. Mix in canned tomatoes, purée and either pasta or rice.
2. Cover with a large plate. Cook 15 mins at full power, stirring 3 times. Pour in two-thirds of the boiling water. Cover as above.
3. Cook 20–25 mins at full power, stirring 4 times. Remove from cooker and stir in rest of water with salt. If soup is too thick for personal taste, add an extra ¼ pt/150 ml boiling water.
4. Ladle into dishes and pass grated Parmesan cheese separately.

CREAM OF CARROT SOUP

2 level tablespoons cornflour

1 large can (about 1¼ lb or 575 g) carrots

¾ pt/425 ml milk (skimmed if liked)

1 level teaspoon onion salt

1 level teaspoon salt

¼–½ pt/150–275 ml extra boiling water

serves 6 (F)

1. Put cornflour into a 4 pt/2.25 litre glass or pottery dish. Mix smoothly with liquid from can of carrots.
2. Blend carrots to a purée in a food processor, blender goblet or by rubbing through a fine mesh sieve. Add to dish with milk and both the salts.
3. Leave uncovered and cook 12 minutes at full power, stirring 4 times. By this time, the soup should have come to the boil and thickened.
4. Remove from oven and thin down to taste with the boiling water. Adjust seasoning to taste and serve straight away.

CHILLED CREAM OF CHESHIRE SOUP
Illustrated on page 17

1 oz/25 g butter or margarine

6 oz/175 g onions, peeled and chopped

3 oz/75 g celery stalks, scrubbed and chopped

1 oz/25 g plain flour

1½ pt/850 ml warm chicken stock

3 tablespoons dry white wine

seasoning to taste

4 oz/125 g blue Cheshire cheese, crumbled

4 oz/125 g white Cheshire cheese, crumbled

¼ pt/150 ml double cream

finely chopped parsley to garnish

serves 6 to 8

1. Put butter or margarine into a 4 pt/2.5 litre glass or pottery dish. Melt, uncovered, 1–1½ mins at defrost setting.
2. Add onions and celery. Mix in well. Cover with a plate and cook 8 mins at full power.
3. Remove from oven. Stir in flour then gradually blend in the stock and wine. Cover as above and return to oven. Cook 10–12 mins at full power, whisking every 2–3 mins to keep mixture smooth.
4. Remove from oven and season to taste. Add cheeses and stir until melted. Leave soup until cold. Blend to a smooth purée in blender goblet. Pour into large bowl and whisk in two-thirds of the cream.
5. Cover and chill several hours or overnight. Before serving, stir round gently to mix then pour into bowls. Swirl in rest of cream and sprinkle each with parsley.

TIP *If soup is too thick after cream has been added, thin down with a little cold milk*

OMELET FU YUNG

Teams well with rice or noodles and microwaved tomato
Illustrated on page 21

½ oz/15 g butter or margarine
3 oz/75 g onion, peeled and finely chopped
2 rounded tablespoons cooked peas
2 rounded tablespoons canned bean sprouts, well-drained
2 oz/50 g trimmed mushrooms, thinly sliced
3 eggs (size 2)
¾ level teaspoon salt
2 tablespoons cold water
1 tablespoon soy sauce
4 spring onions to garnish

serves 2

1. Melt butter or margarine, uncovered, in an 8 in/20 cm shallow round dish. Allow ¾ min at defrost setting.
2. Mix in onion. Cover dish with plate then cook 2 mins at full power. Uncover and stir in peas, bean sprouts and mushrooms.
3. Cover as above and cook 1½ mins. Remove from oven. Beat eggs very thoroughly with salt, water and soy sauce.
4. Pour evenly over ingredients in dish. Cook 5 mins, uncovered, at full power, turning twice unless oven has a turntable.
5. Stand 1 min, cut into 2 portions and transfer to warm plates. Garnish with spring onions. Serve straight away.

OMELET IN PIZZA STYLE

½ oz/15 g butter or margarine
3 eggs (size 2)
3 tablespoons milk
½ level teaspoon salt
12 oz/350 g blanched and skinned tomatoes, sliced
4 oz/125 g Mozzarella cheese, sliced
8 canned anchovies in oil
8 black olives

serves 2

1. Melt butter or margarine, uncovered, in an 8 in/20 cm shallow round dish. Allow ¾ min at defrost setting.
2. Beat eggs very thoroughly with milk and salt. Pour into dish. Cover with plate. Cook 1½ mins at full power. Turn dish half round unless oven has a turntable.
3. Uncover then stir mixture gently with a wooden spoon or fork, bringing the partially set edges to the centre. Return to microwave and cover as before. Cook another 1½ mins at full power.
4. Uncover and cook a further ½ min. Spread with tomatoes and cheese then garnish with anchovies and olives. Leave uncovered and cook 4 mins at full power, turning dish twice unless oven has a turntable. Cut into 2 portions and serve while piping hot.

BLUE CHEESE POTATOES

2 medium, old potatoes, in their jackets
A little butter or margarine and cold milk
1 level teaspoon mustard
2 oz/50 g blue cheese, mashed or crumbled
Seasoning

serves 2 (F)

1. Wash and dry potatoes thoroughly. Slit skin of each potato horizontally. Stand on plate or kitchen paper and cover with more kitchen paper. Cook on full power for 6½–8 mins. Turn 2–3 times during cooking. Stand for 5 mins wrapped in a tea towel.
2. Cut each potato in half following slits.
3. Scoop insides into a bowl and mash finely. Cream until light with sufficient butter or margarine and milk and season to taste. Mix in cheese and mustard.
4. Return mixture to potato shells, put on a plate, cover with kitchen paper and reheat 2¾–3¼ mins at full power.

BUCK RAREBIT

4 oz/125 g Cheddar cheese, finely grated

1 level teaspoon powdered mustard

1 level teaspoon cornflour

1 egg yolk

2 teaspoons milk

salt and pepper to taste

6 tablespoons hot water

1½ teaspoons mild vinegar

3 eggs (size 3)

3 large slices freshly made brown or white toast

paprika

serves 3

1. Mix cheese with mustard, cornflour, egg yolk and milk. Season to taste.
2. Pour 2 tablespoons hot water into each of 3 small glass or pottery dishes. Add ½ teaspoon of vinegar to each to prevent the whites from spreading. Carefully break an egg into each.
Cook 2–2½ mins at full power. Stand for 2 mins.
3. Spread cheese mixture over 3 slices of toast.
4. Leave rarebits uncovered and cook 1 min each at full power.
5. If egg whites are too runny, cook for an extra 20–30 seconds. Remove from dishes with a slotted spoon and place one on top of each rarebit.
Sprinkle very lightly with paprika and serve imediately.

RAREBIT BEANS

PER SERVING
1 large slice fresh toast

butter or margarine

4 rounded tablespoons canned baked beans in tomato sauce

1 oz/25 g grated cheese

1. Stand toast on a plate and spread with butter or margarine. Top with baked beans and sprinkle with grated cheese.
2. Leave uncovered and cook 1¾–2¼ mins at full power.

TORTILLA

½ oz/15 g butter or margarine

4 oz/125 g onions, peeled and finely chopped

6 oz/175 g cold cooked potatoes, cubed

3 eggs (size 2)

¾–1 level teaspoon salt

2 tablespoons cold water

serves 2

1. Melt butter or margarine, uncovered, in an 8 in/20 cm shallow round dish. Allow ¾ min at defrost setting.
2. Mix in onions. Cover dish with plate then cook 2 mins at full power. Uncover and stir in potatoes. Cover again with a plate and cook a further min at full power. Remove from oven.
3. Beat eggs very thoroughly with salt and cold water. Pour evenly over onions and potatoes in dish. Cook, uncovered, for 4½ mins at full power, turning dish twice unless oven has a turntable.
4. Stand 1 min, cut into 2 portions and transfer to warm plates. Serve straight away.

NUT CAKE

4 oz/125 g shelled but unskinned whole almonds, washed and dried

6oz/175 g brazil nuts

2 oz/50 g unsalted peanuts toasted in the microwave. 4–5 mins, full power

4 oz/125 g fresh brown breadcrumbs (soft)

3 oz/75 g onion, peeled and grated

½ level teaspoon salt

1 level teaspoon prepared mustard

1 oz/25 g butter or margarine, melted 1–1½ mins in microwave

2 tablespoons milk

serves 6–8 (F)

1. Grind nuts finely in blender or food processor. Mix with rest of ingredients.
2. Shape into a round of 7–8 ins/17.5–20 cm on a greased plate. Leave uncovered.
3. Cook 3 mins at full power, stand 5 mins, turn plate round and cook a further 2½ mins at full power. Cut into wedges and serve hot or cold.

SMOKED SALMON QUICHE
Illustrated on page 25

shortcrust pastry made with 6 oz/175 g plain flour and 3 oz/75 g fat etc

1 egg yolk

FILLING
6 oz/175 g Pacific smoked salmon, finely chopped

3 eggs (size 3)

½ pt/275 ml single cream

½ level teaspoon salt

½ level teaspoon finely grated lemon peel

serves 8

1. Roll out pastry fairly thinly and use to line a lightly-greased, 8 in/20 cm round glass or pottery fluted flan dish.
2. Prick well all over with a fork, especially where sides of pastry meet base. Leave uncovered and cook 6 mins at full power, turning dish 4 times unless oven has a turntable.
3. Remove from oven, brush all over with egg yolk to seal holes and cook a further min at full power.
4. Remove from oven and cover base with the chopped salmon.
5. Beat all remaining ingredients well together. Pour into flan over salmon. Cook 10–12 mins at full power or until bubbles just begin to break in the middle.
6. Turn 4 times unless oven has a turntable then remove from oven, cut into wedges and Serve hot, warm or cold.

CHEESE AND BACON QUICHE

Shortcrust pastry made with 6 oz/175 g plain flour and 3 oz/75 g fat etc

1 egg yolk

FILLING
4 oz/125 g bacon

3 eggs (size 3)

½ pt/275 ml single cream

½ level teaspoon salt

½ level teaspoon finely grated lemon peel

2 oz/50 g Red Leicester or Cheshire cheese, grated

serves 8

1. Cook bacon 1½–1¾ mins at full power, covered with kitchen paper. Leave to cool, then chop finely.
2. Roll out pastry fairly thinly and use to line a lightly-greased, 8 in/20 cm round glass or pottery fluted flan dish.
3. Prick well all over with a fork, especially where sides of pastry meet base. Leave uncovered and cook 6 mins at full power, turning dish 4 times unless oven has a turntable.
4. Remove from oven, brush all over with egg yolk to seal holes and cook a further min at full power.
5. Remove from oven and cover base with the bacon.
6. Beat eggs, cream salt and peel well together. Pour into flan over bacon and sprinkle with the cheese. Cook 10–12 mins at full power or until bubbles just begin to break in the middle.
7. Turn 4 times unless oven has a turntable then remove from oven, cut into wedges and serve hot, warm or cold.

ITALIAN TOMATO FANCIES

Another version of stuffed tomatoes, these are based on classic Mozzarella cheese and a well-loved Italian herb – oregano.

Illustrated on page 21

6 medium tomatoes
3 oz/75 g fresh brown breadcrumbs
6 oz/175 g firm Mozzarella cheese, grated
½ level teaspoon oregano
½ level teaspoon basil
½ level teaspoon salt
1 garlic clove, peeled and crushed
1 egg (size 4) beaten

serves 6

1. Halve tomatoes and scoop centres into a bowl, discarding hard cores. Stand tomato halves upside-down to drain on kitchen paper.
2. Tip all remaining ingredients into a bowl. Strain in tomato pulp then fork-stir to mix.
3. Pile into tomato halves. Arrange in 2 rings, one inside the other, round the edge of a large plate.
4. Leave uncovered and cook 7–8 mins at full power, turning plate 4 times unless oven has a turntable. Serve hot or cold, allowing 2 halves per person.

NEAPOLITAN BAKED EGG

SAUCE
1½ lb/675 g blanched tomatoes, skinned and cut into eighths
1 garlic clove, peeled and sliced
2 level tablespoons tubed or canned tomato purée
3 level teaspoons caster or soft brown sugar
½ level teaspoon salt
1 level teaspoon dried basil
1 heaped tablespoon chopped parsley
1 level tablespoon cornflour
1 tablespoon cold water
1 egg (size 3) per serving
melted butter or margarine

enough for 6–8 eggs

1. Put tomatoes, garlic and purée into food processor or blender goblet and run machine until smooth.
2. Pour into a 3 pt/1.75 litre glass or pottery dish. Mix in sugar, salt, basil and parsley.
3. Blend cornflour smoothly with water. Add to tomato mixture and stir in well.
4. Cover with plate and cook 6 mins at full power, stirring 4 times.
For each egg
5. Brush a small ramekin or baby soufflé dish with melted butter or margarine. Add 1 generous tablespoon of sauce.
6. Gently break an egg on top of the sauce. Puncture yolk twice with the tip of a knife. Season to taste.
Cover with a saucer and cook 3 minutes at defrost setting. Stand 1 minute.

POTTED HADDOCK

8 oz/225 g unsalted butter
10 oz/275 g cooked smoked haddock (or cod) fillets, skinned and boned
3 teaspoons lemon juice
⅛ level teaspoon nutmeg
½ level teaspoon paprika
GARNISH
6 watercress sprigs

serves 6 (F)

1. Melt 6 oz/175 g butter in a dish for 3 mins at defrost setting. Leave uncovered.
2. Coarsely mash fish and add to butter with the lemon juice, nutmeg and paprika. Leave in the cool until mixture just begins to firm up.
3. Spread neatly and smoothly into 6 baby pots or dishes. Chill until firm in the refrigerator.
4. Melt rest of butter and spoon over each. Chill again until butter has set in an even layer.
5. To serve, run a knife dipped in hot water round inside of each pot, and invert on to a plate. Garnish with watercress and eat with hot toast.

Chilled Cream of Cheshire Soup
Recipe on page 12

Rustic Tomato Soup
Recipe on page 11

AVOCADO FARCI

Perfect for vegetarians, this avocado dish is both unusual and delicious

2 medium to large avocados, fully ripe but not squashy
juice of ½ medium lemon
2 oz/50 g brown breadcrumbs
1½ oz/40 g onion, peeled and finely grated
4 oz/125 g blanched tomatoes, skinned and chopped
2 oz/50 g Lancashire cheese, crumbled or grated
paprika
8 toasted hazelnuts

serves 2 as a snack
serves 4 as a starter

1. Halve avocados and carefully spoon flesh into a bowl. Add lemon juice and mash very finely with a fork.
2. Stir in crumbs, onion and tomatoes. Return to avocado shells and sprinkle with cheese and paprika. Top each with 2 hazelnuts.
3. Arrange on a plate with pointed ends towards centre. Cook, uncovered, for 5 to 5½ mins at full power, turning plate twice unless oven has a turntable. Serve straight away.

VEAL STUFFED PEPPERS

Can be served hot or cold, basted with juices from the dish for added succulence

4 medium red or green peppers (each 4 oz/ 125 g)
1 oz/25 g butter or margarine, at kitchen temperature
5 oz/150 g onions, peeled and chopped
8 oz/225 g minced veal
2 oz/50 g easy-cook, long grain rice
1 level teaspoon salt
5 tablespoons tomato juice, chicken stock or water
½ level teaspoon dried thyme
COOKING LIQUID
4 tablespoons tomato juice or chicken stock

serves 4, allowing 1 per person (F)

1. Wash and dry peppers. Cut off tops and set aside for lids. Remove inside seeds and fibres. Cut a sliver off the base of each so that it stands upright without falling.
2. Put butter or margarine into a dish and heat, uncovered, for ¾–1 min at full power. Stir in onions. Continue to cook, still uncovered, for 3 mins. Mash in veal and cook another 3 mins.
3. Remove from oven and add all remaining ingredients. Spoon equal amounts into peppers. Top with lids.
4. Stand upright in 3 pt/1.75 litre deep dish. Add cooking liquid. Cover with cling film, then puncture twice with the tip of a knife. Alternatively, cover with a matching lid.
5. Cook 15 mins at full power, turning twice unless oven has a turntable. Leave to stand 10 mins. Serve hot or cold, coated with juices from dish.

MUSHROOMS À LA GRÈCQUE

2 bouquet garni bags
1 garlic clove, peeled and crushed
1 large bay leaf, broken into 4 pieces
2 tablespoons water
1 tablespoon lemon juice
1 tablespoon malt vinegar
1 tablespoon corn oil
½ level teaspoon salt
8 oz/225 g button mushrooms, washed and gently wiped dry
1 rounded tablespoon chopped parsley

serves 2

1. Put all ingredients, except mushrooms and parsley, into a medium glass or pottery bowl.
2. Cover with a plate and cook 2½ mins at full power.
3. Gently toss in mushrooms. Cover as above. Cook 3 mins at full power, turning dish twice unless oven has a turntable.
4. Remove from oven and leave until cold. Lift mushrooms into a dish. Coat with juices, strained through a fine mesh sieve.
5. Chill several hours before serving. Transfer mushrooms and juices to 2 dishes and sprinkle with parsley.

AVOCADO HOLLANDAISE

A very rich combination for a classic dish

4 oz/125 g slightly salted butter

1 tablespoon fresh lemon juice

2 size 3 egg yolks

salt and pepper to taste

pinch of caster sugar

3 firm avocados

serves 6

1. Put butter into a smallish jug or dish and leave uncovered. Melt until hot and bubbly for 1 to 1½ mins at full power.
2. Add lemon juice and egg yolks. Whisk well. Return to oven and cook 30 seconds at full power.
3. Remove from oven and stir briskly. The sauce is ready if it is thick as cold custard and clings to whisk, fork or spoon – whichever implement you have used. If not, cook a further 15 seconds.
4. Season with salt and pepper to taste, then add sugar to counteract sharpness coming from the lemon.
5. Halve avocados and remove stones. Fill each halve with warm Hollandaise sauce and serve immediately.

LIVER PASTE

6 oz/175 g salted butter

1 garlic clove, peeled and sliced

1 lb/450 g chicken livers, washed, dried, and
   each piece punctured

⅛ level teaspoon nutmeg

seasoning to taste

about 2–3 oz/50–75 g extra butter for the top

serves about 10 to 12 (F)

1. Put butter into a 3 pt/1.75 litre dish and heat 2 mins, uncovered, at full power.
2. Add garlic and chicken livers. Cover with cling film, then puncture twice with the tip of a knife.
3. Cook 8 mins at full power, turning dish 4 times unless oven has a turntable.
4. Remove from microwave then add nutmeg and seasoning to taste. Spoon butter and cooked liver together into a food processor or blender goblet. Do this in 2 batches and run machine each time until mixture is very smooth.
5. Spread evenly into a smallish, soufflé-type dish. For an airtight seal (the best there is) melt extra butter and pour over the top. Leave, without moving, until butter sets then 'store', covered, in the refrigerator.
6. To serve, spoon out on to plates and serve with hot toast.

MAIN DISHES:
SOMETHING SPECIAL

BEEF AND MUSHROOM KEBABS WITH BROWN RICE

BROWN RICE

4 oz/125 g brown rice
1 level teaspoon salt
1¾ pt/1 litre boiling water

KEBABS

24 dried bay leaves
6 tablespoons water
1½ lb/675 g rump steak
6 oz/175 g button mushrooms
½ green pepper (2 oz/50 g), washed and de-seeded
½ red pepper (2 oz/50 g), washed and de-seeded
2 oz/50 g butter or margarine, at kitchen temperature
1 level teaspoon paprika

serves 4

1. To cook rice, put all ingredients into a 3½ pt/2 litre glass or pottery dish and stand on a plate in case water boils over.
2. Stir round to mix. Cover with cling film, then puncture twice with the tip of a knife. Alternatively, cover with matching lid.
3. Cook 30 mins at full power, turning 4 times unless oven has a turntable. Leave to stand 10 mins inside or outside the oven, whichever is the most convenient. Uncover and drain.
4. Fluff up by stirring with a fork. Set aside and keep warm.
5. Put bay leaves into a small bowl, add water and cover with a saucer. Heat for 2 mins at full power to soften, otherwise the leaves will break. (Dried leaves are very brittle.) If you have a bay tree in the garden, use fresh leaves.
6. Trim fat off steak and discard. Cut meat into ¾ in/about 2 cm cubes. Wash and trim mushrooms and wipe dry.
7. Cut both peppers into smallish squares, put into a dish and only just cover with water. Top with an inverted plate and heat for 1 min to soften.
8. Drain bay leaves and peppers. Thread steak, mushrooms, pepper squares and bay leaves on to 12 metal skewers (or wooden ones if available), each 4 in/10 cm long.
9. Arrange, like spokes of a wheel, in a 10 in/25 cm round and shallow glass or pottery dish.
10. Put butter or margarine into a cup, cover with a saucer and melt for 1½–2 mins at defrost setting. Stir in paprika.
11. Brush over kebabs. Cook, uncovered, for 8 mins at full power, turning dish twice unless oven has a turntable.
12. Twist kebabs round and brush undersides with rest of butter mixture. Cook a further 4 mins at full power, turning dish twice.
13. Arrange on a bed of rice and coat with gravy from dish. Allow 3 skewers per person.

BUFFET MEAT SLICE
Can be served hot or cold

2 lb/900 g raw minced beef, as lean as possible
2 eggs (size 2) beaten
1 brown gravy cube
2 level teaspoons onion salt
4 level tablespoons plain flour
2 rounded tablespoons tomato ketchup
2 level teaspoons mixed herbs
2 teaspoons soy sauce

FOR GARNISH:
glacé cherries, black olives and mint leaves

serves 8 to 10 (F)

1. Tip meat into a mixing bowl and work in beaten eggs, crumbled gravy cube, onion salt, flour, ketchup and herbs.
2. Spread into a 2 pt/1.25 litre oblong greased dish that resembles a loaf tin.
3. Brush top gently with soy sauce. Cover with cling film, then puncture twice with the tip of a knife.
4. Cook 5 mins at full power. Leave to stand in the oven for 5 mins. Continue to cook a further 10 mins at defrost setting, turning dish 4 times unless oven has a turntable.
5. Stand 5 mins. Uncover. Carefully drain off surplus fat from container then carefully lift the Meat Slice on to a dish.
6. Garnish with pieces of glacé cherries, black olives and a few mint leaves and serve hot or cold.

Italian Tomato Fancies
Recipe on page 16

Omelet Fu-Yung
Recipe on page 13

BUFFET MEATBALL CURRY

RICE

4 oz/125 g brown rice

1 level teaspoon salt

1¾/1 litre boiling water

MEATBALLS

1½ lb/675 g minced beef

2 oz/50 g fresh white breadcrumbs

½ level teaspoon onion or garlic salt

1 egg (size 2) beaten

1 can condensed cream of tomato soup

1 lb/450 g peeled and chopped tomatoes

2 teaspoons soy sauce

1 level tablespoon mild curry powder (or more
     to taste)

1 level tablespoon tubed or canned tomato purée

1 crumbled brown gravy cube

3 rounded tablespoons mango chutney

serves 8

1. To cook rice, put all ingredients into a 3½
pt/2 litre glass or pottery dish and stand on a
plate in case water boils over.
2. Stir round to mix. Cover with cling film,
then puncture twice with the tip of the knife.
Alternatively, cover with matching lid.
3. Cook 30 mins at full power, turning 4
times unless oven has a turntable. Leave to
stand 10 mins inside or outside the oven,
whichever is the most convenient. Uncover
and drain.
4. Fluff up by stirring with a fork. Set aside
and keep warm.
5. Mix together mince, crumbs, onion or
garlic salt and egg. Shape into 16 balls and
arrange round the edge of a 10 × 2 in/
25 × 5 cm round glass or pottery dish.
6. Mix remaining ingredients together and
spooon into dish, making sure the meatballs
have their fair share and are well coated.
7. Cover with cling film, then puncture
twice with the tip of a knife. Alternatively,
cover dish with matching lid.
8. Cook 18 mins at full power, turning dish
4 times unless oven has a turntable.
9. Leave to stand 5 mins then uncover and
baste meatballs with tomato mixture. Adjust
seasoning to taste. Reheat, uncovered, for 1½
mins at full power. Serve with rice and salad.
Also extra chutney if liked.

ARTICHOKES FARCI

*Team with new potatoes cooked in their skins and delicate
mange-tout, tossed in melted butter and very lightly
seasoned with a trace of basil, chopped fresh for preference,
otherwise dried.*

4 large globe artichokes

¼ pt/150 ml dry red wine

1 garlic clove

1 rounded teaspoon salt

1 lb/450 g raw minced beef, as lean as possible

6 oz/175 g onions, peeled and finely chopped

1 egg (size 3) beaten

1 level teaspoon mixed dried herbs

1½ level teaspoons salt

1 teaspoon Worcestershire sauce

2 tablespoons water

¼ pt/150 ml tomato or vegetable juice such as
     V8

serves 4 (F)

1. To cook artichokes, cut away stalks,
leaving bases flat. With a sharp and non-
serrated knife, cut tops off upper leaves as
though you were slicing a loaf of bread. You
will find the easiest way to do this is to place
each artichoke on its side.
2. Soak for 20 mins in cold, salted water.
Lift out and shake to remove surplus liquid.
3. Pour wine into a large dish, about 10
inches square by 2 inches in depth (25 cm by
5 cm). Crush in garlic then stir in salt. Add
artichokes, placing them upright with leaves
facing.
4. Cover with cling film, then puncture
twice with the tip of a knife. Alternatively,
cover with a matching lid.
5. Cook 25 mins at full power, turning dish
4 times unless oven has a turntable. Leave
upside-down in a colander to drain
thoroughly.
6. When completely cold, turn right way up.
Open out leaves and gently remove central
cones. The bristly cores underneath are the
'chokes' and should be plucked out, bit by
bit, with fingers. Left behind will be the
much prized hearts surrounded by layers of
leaves.
7. For stuffing, mix meat with onions, egg,
herbs, salt, Worcestershire sauce and water.
Spoon into artichoke cavities. Tie round with

string. Stand, close together and upright, in a deep glass or pottery dish.

8. Cover with cling film, then puncture twice with the tip of a knife. Alternatively, cover with a matching lid.

9. Cook for 8 mins at full power, turning dish 4 times unless oven has a turntable. Uncover and add tomato or vegetable juice.

10. Re-cover as before. Cook a further 8 mins at full power, turning dish 4 times. Serve hot as suggested above or, if preferred, leave until cold then chill in the refrigerator and serve with salad – blissful on a balmy summer day.

PORK 'N' PINEAPPLE WITH CURRY RICE

Always popular and very much a restaurant favourite, the dish can be microwaved to perfection in 40 mins. I serve it with the mild Curry Rice below and a salad based on watercress, crisp lettuce and diced dessert apples, all tossed in a sharpish dressing. It contrasts beautifully with the mild flavour of the pork and the sweetness of the pineapple.

RICE

1 oz/25 g butter or margarine

10 oz/275 g onion, peeled and grated

8 oz/225 g Basmati rice

1 large bay leaf

cloves

seeds from 4 opened-out cardamom pods

2 rounded tablespoons mild curry powder

1 level teaspoon salt

1 pt/575 ml boiling chicken or vegetable stock

2 rounded tablespoons mango chutney

4 spare rib of pork chops, each 8 oz/225 g and fat trimmed

1 can (15½oz/439 g) pineapple rings in syrup

1 level teaspoon paprika

4 teaspoons soy sauce

½ level teaspoon garlic granules

serves 4 (F)

1. Melt butter or margarine in a 4 pt/2.25 litre glass or pottery dish for 1–1½ mins at defrost setting. Leave uncovered. Add onion. Cook, uncovered, for 5 mins at full power.

2. Stir in remaining rice ingredients. Cover dish with cling film, then puncture twice with the tip of a knife.

3. Cook 18 mins at full power, turning dish 4 times unless oven has a turntable.

4. Leave to stand 8 mins inside or outside the oven, whichever is the most convenient, so that rice grains absorb all the liquid.

5. Wash and dry chops then arrange in a fairly shallow, 10 in/25 cm round glass or pottery dish.

6. Drain pineapple. Reserve 2 tablespoons of the syrup for the baste and keep remainder for drinks or sauces.

7. Arrange pineapple rings over chops. Beat reserved pineapple syrup with all remaining ingredients. Spoon over chops.

8. Cover with cling film, then puncture twice with the tip of a knife. Alternatively, cover with a matching lid.

9. Cook 20 mins at full power, turning dish 4 times unless oven has a turntable. Leave to stand 5 mins. Serve with rice reheated for 3–5 mins at defrost setting.

HONEYED PORK

1 leg of pork

BASTE

4 rounded tablespoons clear honey

1 rounded teaspoon prepared English mustard

1 level teaspoon salt

2 teaspoons Worcestershire sauce

cloves

1. Mix together baste ingredients and brush over scored rind of pork joint.

2. Put into shallow dish. Cover with film and slit twice.
Cook 7 mins per lb/450 g, allowing 5 mins per lb/450 g standing time. This should take place half way through cooking time for large joints with further standing time at end. Smaller joints may be left to stand when cooking time is completed.
Turn dish several times during cooking. When standing at the end, wrap joint in foil. Alternatively, cook and leave to stand in roasting bag.

3. Before serving, stud rind with cloves.

CREAMY CHICKEN AU POIVRE

Teams happily with a green salad and microwaved rice, first forked with butter and enough chopped parsley to turn it a pretty green – about 3 heaped tablespoons.

1 oz/25 g butter or margarine, at kitchen temperature

5 oz/150 g onions, peeled and finely chopped

1 lb/450 g–500 g chicken breast fillets (or use turkey if preferred), washed and dried

1 level tablespoon cornflour

2 tablespoons water

1 level tablespoon tubed or canned tomato purée

3 rounded teaspoons Madagascan green peppercorns, available in cans or glass jars from speciality food shops

1 carton (5 oz/142 ml) soured cream

1 level teaspoon salt

serves 6

1. Put butter or margarine into an 8 × 2 in/ 20 × 5 cm round glass or pottery dish. Melt, uncovered, 1–1½ mins at defrost setting.
2. Stir in onions. Cook, also uncovered, at full power, allowing 2 mins. Leave to stand while preparing chicken. Cut, across the grain, into 1 in/2.5 cm wide strips.
3. Mix well with onions and butter. Cover with a plate or matching lid. Cook 6 mins at full power.
4. Meanwhile, mix cornflour smoothly with water then add purée, green peppercorns, soured cream and salt.
5. Stir into chicken and onions then move mixture to edges of dish to form a hollow in the centre.
6. Cover with cling film (more secure than a plate) then puncture twice with the tip of a knife. Alternatively, cover with matching lid. Cook 8 mins at full power, turning dish 4 times unless oven has a turntable.
7. Leave to stand 5 mins, uncover and stir round before serving.

CHICORY HAM WRAPS IN CHEESE SAUCE

Serve with chips or boiled potatoes

8 heads of chicory (about 2¼ lb/1 kg)

¼ pt/150 ml boiling water mixed with 1 tablespoon lemon juice

8 slices ham (7–8 oz/200–225 g)

1 pt/575 ml milk, taken from the refrigerator

2 oz/50 g butter or margarine

1½ oz/40 g plain flour

4 oz/125 g Gouda cheese, grated

2oz/50 g Double Gloucester cheese, grated

serves 4 generously

1. Trim chicory, removing any outer leaves that are either bruised or damaged. Cut out a cone-shaped core from base of each chicory head as this is very often bitter and can spoil the flavour.
2. Arrange in a 14 in/35 cm oval glass dish or in an oblong dish measuring about 12 × 7½ ins/30 × 19 cm. Coat with water and lemon juice.
3. Cover with cling film, then puncture twice with the tip of a knife. Cook 14 mins at full power, turning dish twice.
4. Stand outside the microwave oven 5 mins. Lift into a colander, drain thoroughly and leave until lukewarm. Wrap a slice of ham round each then return to washed and dried dish in which chicory were originally cooked.
5. Heat milk in an uncovered jug for 3 mins at full power. Leave to stand outside oven. Put butter or margarine into a 2 pt/1.25 litre bowl and melt, uncovered, 2–2½ mins at defrost setting. Stir in flour then gradually whisk in hot milk until mixture is very smooth.
6. Cook for 5–6 mins at full power or until sauce just comes to boil. Beat hard at end of every min. Mix in cheese.
7. Pour over wrapped chicory in dish then cover with cling film as directed above. Reheat 3 mins at full power and stand 5 mins before serving.

Smoked Salmon Quiche
Recipe on page 15

NORMANDY APPLE CHICKEN

Perfect with boiled potatoes tossed in butter and a full blown mixed salad

2 oz/50 g butter or margarine, at kitchen temperature

2 lb/900 g chicken joints, thawed completely if frozen

6 oz/175 g onions, peeled and chopped

8 oz/225 g cooking apples, peeled and finely chopped (cores removed)

1 garlic clove, peeled and chopped (optional)

2 level tablespoons flour

½ pt/275 ml medium cider

2 brown gravy cubes

1 level teaspoon dried thyme

salt and pepper to taste

1 rounded tablespoon chopped parsley

serves 4 (F)

1. Put butter or margarine into a 10 × 2 in/ 25 × 5 cm glass or pottery dish. Leave uncovered and melt 1½–2 mins at defrost setting.
2. Add chicken joints and toss round in the butter or margarine. Cover with cling film then puncture twice with the tip of a knife. Alternatively, cover with a matching lid.
3. Cook 15 mins at full power turning dish 4 times unless oven has a turntable.
4. Uncover then sprinkle onions, apples and garlic (if used) over chicken. Mix flour smoothly with some of the measured cider. Add remainder.
5. Crumble in the 2 gravy cubes then add thyme. Spoon liquid into dish over chicken and vegetables etc. Cover as directed above. Cook 15 mins at full power, turning dish 4 times unless oven has a turntable. Leave to stand 10 mins.
6. Uncover and gently stir round. Adjust seasoning to taste and sprinkle with parsley.

CHICKEN FROM THE FOREST

Serve with freshly microwaved noodles or rice and a selection of vegetables

2½ lb (just over 1 kg) chicken drumsticks

2 tablespoons salad oil or the same amount of melted butter or margarine

6 oz/175 g streaky bacon, chopped

4 oz/125 g onions, peeled and chopped

4 oz/125 g button mushrooms, washed then dried and sliced

10 oz/275 g jar or can tomato sauce for spaghetti

1 tablespoon malt vinegar

1 tablespoon lemon juice

2 level tablespoons light brown soft sugar

1 level teaspoon prepared Continental mustard

2 tablespoons Worcestershire sauce

chopped parsley for garnishing

serves 4 (F)

1. Skin drumsticks and leave on one side temporarily.
2. Pour oil or fat into an oblong glass dish measuring about 14 × 9 ins/35 × 22.5 cm. Heat 1 min at full power, leaving uncovered.
3. Add bacon and onions. Stir well to mix. Cook, uncovered, for 5 mins at full power.
4. Add drumsticks, turning over and over in the bacon and onion mixture. Finally arrange with the thickest parts towards the edge of the dish.
5. Sprinkle with mushrooms. Beat tomato sauce with vinegar, lemon juice, sugar, mustard and Worcestershire sauce. Spoon over chicken.
6. Cover with cling film, then puncture twice with the tip of a knife. Cook 15 mins at full power. Uncover, turn drumsticks over and re-cover with film. Puncture.
7. Continue to cook for a further 15 mins at full power. Remove from oven, leave to stand 5 mins, uncover and sprinkle with parsley.

LIVER AND BACON

A special attraction main course made from those tubs of frozen chicken livers now readily available from supermarket chains.

6 oz/175 g onions, peeled and sliced

8 oz/225 g streaky bacon, de-rinded and chopped

1 lb/450 g chicken livers (2 tubs), defrosted if frozen then rinsed and well-drained

3 level tablespoons cornflour

4 tablespoons cold water

$\frac{1}{4}$ pt/150 ml boiling water

1–1$\frac{1}{2}$ level teaspoons salt (care here as bacon may be salty)

pepper to taste

serves 6 (F)

1. Put onions and chopped bacon into a 3 pt/ 1.75 litre glass or pottery dish. Leave uncovered and cook 7 mins at full power, stirring 3 times.
2. Mix in livers, each of which should first be punctured with the tip of knife to prevent popping. Cover with a plate and cook 8 mins at full power, stirring 2 or 3 times. Leave to stand in oven for 5 mins.
3. Mix cornflour smoothly with cold water. Add boiling water and salt then add to livers. Stir thoroughly.
4. Cover with a plate and cook 6 mins at full power, turning dish 3 times unless oven has a turntable.
5. Stir round, season to taste with pepper then serve with creamed potatoes or freshly cooked rice and a selection of vegetables to taste.

WINE POACHED SALMON STEAKS WITH HOLLANDAISE TARTAR

Serve garnished with a slice of lemon and either a frond of dill or a spray of parsley

4 salmon steaks, about 1$\frac{1}{2}$ lb/675 g, thawed if frozen

$\frac{1}{4}$ pt/150 ml dry white wine

$\frac{1}{2}$ level teaspoon salt

SAUCE
4 oz/125 g slightly salted butter

1 tablespoon fresh lemon juice

2 egg yolks (size 3)

1 tablespoon chopped gherkins

1 tablespoon chopped parsley

1 tablespoon capers, drained and chopped

$\frac{1}{2}$ level teaspoon grated lemon peel

serves 4

1. Arrange salmon steaks round the edge of an 8 in/20 cm round and shallow glass or pottery dish.
2. Pour wine into centre then sprinkle fish with salt. Cover with cling film, then puncture twice with the tip of a knife. Alternatively cover with matching lid.
3. Cook for 8 mins at full power, turning dish 4 times unless oven has a turntable.
4. Remove from microwave and leave to stand 5 mins. Lift out of dish with slatted fish slice and transfer to warm plates. Garnish and accompany with sauce.
5. To make the sauce, put butter into a smallish jug or dish and leave uncovered. Melt until hot and bubbly for 1–1$\frac{1}{2}$ mins at full power.
6. Add lemon juice and egg yolks. Whisk well. Return to oven and cook 30 secs at full power.
7. Remove from oven and stir briskly. The sauce is ready if it is thick as cold custard and clings to spoon. If not, cook a further 15 secs.
8. Stir in remaining ingredients and serve.

MONK FISH WITH EGG AND LEMON SAUCE

1½ lb/675 g monk fish

1 oz/25 g butter, at kitchen temperature

3 level tablespoons plain flour

½ pt/275 ml milk, warmed for 2 mins at full
  power

2 egg yolks (size 2)

juice of 1 large lemon (about 6 oz/175 g)

½–1 level teaspoon salt

2 rounded tablespoons chopped chives, green
  part of leek or parsley

serves 6

1. Cut monk fish away from bone then divide flesh into scampi-sized pieces with a sharp and non-serrated knife. Wash and dry.
2. Put butter into an 8 × 12 in/20 × 50 cm round glass or pottery dish. Leave uncovered and melt 1–1½ mins at defrost setting.
3. Coat pieces of monk fish with flour then add to dish of butter. Toss round until well-coated. Mix in milk.
4. Cover with cling film, then puncture twice with the tip of a knife.
5. Cook 7 mins at full power, turning dish 4 times unless oven has a turntable.
6. Meanwhile, beat yolks and lemon juice well together. Season with salt. Add to fish at the end of its cooking time. Stir in well.
7. Cook a further 2 mins at full power then leave to stand 5 mins. Stir round, sprinkle with greenery and serve with plain boiled rice or new potatoes. French beans go well with the fish.

MAIN DISHES: SOMETHING SIMPLE

TOMATO BEEF 'CAKE'

Teams happily with creamy mash and green vegetables to taste

10 oz/275 g raw minced beef, as lean as
  possible

1 oz/25 g plain flour

1 egg (size 3)

1 level teaspoon onion salt

¼ pt/150 ml tomato juice

1 teaspoon soy sauce

1 level teaspoon mixed herbs

serves 2 to 3 (F)

1. Well-grease a 1½ pt/about 1 litre oval pie dish.
2. Mix beef with all remaining ingredients and spread smoothly into dish.
3. Cover with cling film, then puncture twice with knife tip.
4. Cook for 7 mins at full power, turning dish twice unless oven has turntable. Leave to stand 5 mins inside or outside the oven, whichever is the most convenient.
5. Uncover. Lift out on to a warm plate with 2 spatulas, leaving behind surplus fat in dish which may have seeped out during cooking. Cut loaf into 2 or 3 portions and serve.

CHILLI PORK CHOPS
Serve piping hot and steaming, with jacket potatoes and sprouts

4 spare ribs of pork chops, (each 8 oz/225 g) and fat trimmed
2 level teaspoons chilli seasoning
1 level teaspoon onion salt
1 can (14 oz/400 g) red kidney beans, drained
1 can (14 oz/400 g) tomatoes, coarsely crushed

serves 4 (F)

1. Arrange chops in an 8 in/20 cm square glass or pottery dish. Sprinkle with chilli seasoning.
2. Cover with cling film, then puncture twice with the tip of a knife. Alternatively, cover with a matching lid.
3. Cook for 8 mins at full power, turning dish 4 times unless oven has a turntable.
4. Uncover. Sprinkle with salt then top with beans and contents of can of tomatoes. Re-cover as before.
5. Cook 15 mins at full power. Stand 5 mins then serve as suggested above.

BUTTER BEAN AND BEEF STEW WITH TOMATOES

1 can (15 oz/425 g) butter beans, drained

1 can (10.6 oz or 300 g) ready-to-serve cream of tomato soup

1 rounded tablespoon dried chopped onions

6 slices of feather steak (about 1¼ lb/575 g)

salt and pepper to taste

serves 6 (F)

1. Combine butter beans, soup and onions together in an 8 × 2 in/20 × 5 cm round glass or pottery dish.
2. Cover with a plate. Cook 6 mins at full power, turning dish 3 times unless oven has a turntable.
3. Uncover and stir to mix. Arrange steak in a border round edge of dish. Cover with cling film, then puncture twice with the tip of a knife. Alternatively, cover with matching lid.
4. Cook 15 mins at full power, turning dish 4 times unless oven has a turntable.
5. Leave to stand 10 mins inside or outside the oven, whichever is the most convenient. Season to taste. Serve with creamed potatoes, Brussels sprouts and microwaved carrots tossed in butter and a hint of nutmeg.

VEAL LOAF

Cut the loaf into wedges while still hot and you have a delicious meal with gravy and vegetables. Left to get cold, you can slice the loaf and serve it with salad.

1 lb/450 g raw veal, finely minced

1 garlic clove, peeled and crushed

1 oz/25 g plain flour

2 eggs (size 2) beaten

¼ level teaspoon salt

½ level teaspoon dried thyme

1 teaspoon Worcestershire sauce

grated nutmeg

serves 4 (F)

1. Well-grease an oblong dish measuring 5 × 7 × 2 in/12.5 × 17.5 × 5 cm.
2. Mix veal thoroughly with all remaining ingredients, except nutmeg, then spread into prepared dish.
3. Cover with cling film, then puncture twice with the tip of a knife. Alternatively, cover with matching lid.
4. Cook 8 mins at full power, turning dish 4 times unless oven has a turntable. Remove from oven and take off cling film. Sprinkle Loaf with nutmeg and serve as suggested above.

MILD TURKEY CURRY

If a hotter curry is preferred, add cayenne pepper to taste, allowing from an eighth of a teaspoon to one level – or use a few drops of Tabasco. Chicken may be substituted for turkey.

1 oz/25 g butter or margarine, at kitchen temperature

5 oz/150 g onions, peeled and very thinly sliced

1 garlic clove, peeled and crushed

1 oz/25 g raisins

1 oz/25 g desiccated coconut

1 oz/25 g flour

3 rounded teaspoons Madras curry powder

½ pt/275 ml boiling water

2 tablespoons milk

¼ level teaspoon salt

3 teaspoons fresh lemon juice

12 oz/350 g cooked turkey, removed from bones and diced

serves 4 (F)

1. Put butter or margarine into an 8 × 2 in/ 20 × 5 cm round dish. Melt, uncovered, for about 1–1½ mins at defrost setting.
2. Stir in onions, garlic, raisins and coconut. Leave uncovered and cook 2 mins at full power.
3. Mix in flour, curry powder, water, milk, salt, lemon juice and turkey. Cover with cling film then puncture twice with the tip of a knife. Alternatively, cover with a matching lid.
4. Cook 6 mins at full power, turning dish 4 times unless oven has a turntable. Leave to stand 5 mins inside or outside the oven, whichever is the most convenient.
5. Uncover, stir round, transfer to a warm dish and serve with freshly cooked rice, mango chutney and a salad of sliced onions, separated into rings, with thinly sliced red or green pepper. If liked, also serve a dish of plain yogurt sprinkled with chopped preserved ginger.

'BARBECUED' RIB BONES WITH NOODLES

Serve with a fresh salad made from bean sprouts and thinly sliced raw mushrooms tossed in French dressing

PASTA
8oz/225 g dry noodles (break spaghetti into thirds)

1 level teaspoon salt

2 teaspoons salad oil

BASTE
2 oz/50 g butter or margarine, at room temperature

1 level tablespoon tomato ketchup

2 teaspoons soy sauce

1 level teaspoon paprika

¼ teaspoon garlic granules

½ teaspoon chilli sauce (hot)

RIBS
2 lb/1 kg fleshy pork rib bones (sheet ribs or spare rib bones)

serves 4

1. Put noodles into a large glass or pottery dish. Add 1½ pt/850 ml boiling water, salt and salad oil to prevent the pasta from sticking together.
Leave uncovered and cook 12–15 mins at full power, stirring gently 4 times.
Remove from oven, cover and leave to stand for another 6–8 mins or until pasta swells and absorbs most of the liquid.
2. Keep warm.
3. To make baste, melt butter or margarine, uncovered, for about 1½–2 mins at defrost setting. Stir in all remaining ingredients. Leave on one side.
4. Divide pork bones into single ribs then wash well and dry with kitchen paper. Arrange in a large dish with narrow part of bones pointing inwards.
5. Cover with cling film, then puncture twice with the tip of a knife.
6. Cook for 10 mins at full power, turning dish 4 times unless oven has a turntable. Remove cling film, pour off fat then brush bones with baste, using about half the quantity.

7. Leave uncovered and cook 3 mins at full power. Turn ribs over and brush with remaining baste. Cook, uncovered, a further 2 mins.
8. Drain noodles, arrange on 4 large plates then place ribs on top.

TURKEY FLAN

Hot or cold, this is an appetising flan. It responds well to an accompaniment of salad or cauliflower cheese.

BASE
shortcrust pastry made with 6 oz/175 g plain flour, 3 oz/75 g fat etc

FILLING
12 oz/350 g cold cooked turkey, cut into large cubes or strips

4 oz/125 g onion, peeled and cut into eighths

2 eggs (size 3) beaten

5 tablespoons cold milk

1 scant level teaspoon salt

white pepper to taste

GARNISH
sliced onion, separated into rings

chopped parsley

serves 6 to 8

1. Roll out pastry on floured surface and use to line a greased, round pie plate with rim. It should be about 7½ inches in diameter at the top, sloping downwards to 6½ inches (about 19–16 cm). The depth should be about 1½ ins/4 cm.
2. Prick well all over, especially where base of pastry meets sides. Bake, uncovered, for 6 mins at full power, turning 4 times unless oven has a turntable. Remove from oven and gently press down any bulges with hand protected by oven glove.
3. For filling, finely mince turkey and onion. Transfer to mixing bowl then add eggs, milk, salt and pepper. Mix thoroughly and spread smoothly into pastry case.
4. Cook, uncovered, 7½–8 mins (or until filling is firm and set), at full power, turning dish 4 times unless oven has a turntable.
5. Leave to stand 5 mins inside or outside the oven, whichever is the most convenient. Garnish with a border of onion rings then sprinkle with parsley. Cut into wedges and serve hot or cold.

RICE AND TURKEY TUMBLE

What better way of using up leftover turkey – or indeed any other cold roast meat – than in this uncomplicated dish which is geared for family eating. It conveniently uses store cupboard ingredients.

8 oz/225 g easy cook, long grain rice

1 can condensed cream of celery soup

½ pt/275 ml boiling water

1 can (11½ oz/329 g) sweetcorn, undrained

8 oz/225 g cold cooked turkey, cubed

serves 4 generously

1. Put rice into a 3 pt/1.75 litre dish. Blend in soup and water.
2. When evenly mixed, add rest of ingredients and stir in well.
3. Cover with matching lid or cling film, puncturing the latter twice with the tip of knife.
4. Cook for 25 mins at full power, turning dish 4 times unless oven has a turntable.
5. Uncover, stir round and spoon out on to warm plates to serve. Accompany with a salad or cooked vegetables to taste.

PEANUT CHICKEN

Teams well with those Chinese-style noodles available from most supermarkets

2 lb/900 g chicken joints

4 oz/125 g smooth peanut butter

½ level teaspoon ground ginger

½ level teaspoon onion salt

1 rounded teaspoon medium strength Madras curry powder

Chinese barbecue sauce (Hoi Sin)

serves 4 (F)

1. Arrange joints, in a single layer, around the edge of a 10 in/25 cm round dish which is fairly shallow.
2. Put peanut butter into a small dish. Leave uncovered and heat 1 min at defrost setting.
3. Stir in ginger, onion salt and curry powder. Spread over joints.
4. Top each with a little barbecue sauce (Hoi Sin). Cover with cling film, then puncture twice with the tip of a knife.
5. Cook 16 mins at full power, turning dish 4 times unless oven has a turntable. Stand 5 mins before serving.

SWEET-SOUR DUCKLING WITH BEAN SPROUTS

Goes well with freshly cooked noodles tossed with peas and strips of omelet

1 × 4½ lb/2 kg duckling, thawed and weighed after giblets have been removed

2 slightly rounded tablespoons mango chutney

BEAN SPROUTS
1 lb/450 g fresh bean sprouts

2 teaspoons soy sauce

1 teaspoon Worcestershire sauce

1 level teaspoon onion salt

serves 4

1. Keep giblets from duckling and use for conventionally cooked soup such as vegetable broth or Minestrone.
2. Wash bird inside and out under cold, running water.
3. Place a plastic rack or 2 inverted saucers into an oblong dish measuring about 12 × 7½ in/30 × 19 cm. Stand duck on top, breast side down.
4. Cover with cling film, then puncture twice with the tip of a knife.
5. Cook 20 mins at full power, turnng dish 4 times unless oven has a turntable.
6. Uncover. Turn duckling over carefully, using 2 wooden spoons, so that breast side is now uppermost.
7. Spread thickly with the chutney then re-cover with cling film as before. Cook a further 20 mins, turning as above. Leave to stand 10 mins.
8. To cook the bean sprouts: Toss all the ingredients well together in a bowl. Transfer to an 8 in/20 cm round glass or pottery dish that is fairly deep.
9. Cover with cling film, then puncture twice with the tip of a knife.
10. Cook 5 mins at full power, turning dish twice unless oven has a turntable. Uncover, stir round and serve with the duckling.

FRENCH COUNTRY LIVER WITH CASSEROLED LEEKS

An absolute winner for those who enjoy offal, and liver in particular. Rice is the best partner.

LEEKS

4–5 narrow leeks (1 lb/450–500 g)

1 oz/25 g melted butter mixed with 4 tablespoons chicken stock

salt and pepper

LIVER

1 oz/25 g butter or margarine

6 oz/175 g onions, peeled and finely chopped or grated

1 lb/450 g lambs liver, cut into strips measuring 4 × 1 in/10 × 2.5 cm

1 rounded tablespoon plain flour

½ pt/275 ml dry red wine

2 rounded teaspoons dark brown sugar

1 brown gravy cube, crumbled

1 rounded tablespoon parsley

seasoning to taste

serves 4–6

1. Slit, well wash and chop the leeks. Put into a 3 pt/1.75 litre dish. Add melted butter or margarine with chicken stock and seasoning.
2. Cover with matching lid or cling film punctured twice and cook 10 mins at full power. Keep warm.
3. Put butter or margarine into a 10 in/ 25 cm fairly shallow round dish and melt 1–1½ mins at defrost setting. Leave uncovered.
4. Stir in onions and liver. Cover with a plate and cook 5 mins at full power.
5. Mix in all remaining ingredients except seasoning. Cover with a plate as before and cook 6 mins at full power, stirring mixture twice.
6. Leave to stand 3 mins then uncover, stir round and season to taste. Serve with drained leeks first reheated for 2–3 mins at defrost setting.

PLAICE WITH CELERY CREAM SAUCE

Serve the plaice with brown rice or brown pasta, and a fresh green salad tingling with French dressing

2 level tablespoons desiccated coconut

8 plaice fillets (about 2 lb/900 g), washed and dried

1 can condensed cream of celery soup

¼ pt/150 ml boiling water

¼ level teaspoon marjoram

serves 4

1. Spread coconut on to a 10 in/25 cm pottery plate or put into a 7 in/17.5 cm round glass dish. Leave uncovered. Toast in the microwave for 3–4 mins at full power or until coconut is light golden brown. Move about with a wooden spoon or fork at the end of every min. Remove from oven but leave on the plate or in the dish so that it goes on gently cooking and crispening.
2. Wash and dry fish then roll up each fillet from head end to tail, flesh sides outside.
3. Arrange in a 10 in/25 cm round shallow dish, first brushed with butter or margarine.
4. Whisk soup and water well together. Stir in marjoram then spoon over fish.
5. Sprinkle with coconut. Cover with cling film, then puncture twice with the tip of a knife.
6. Cook 12 mins at full power, turning dish 4 times unless oven has a turntable. Leave to stand 5 mins inside or outside the oven, whichever is the most convenient.
7. Continue to cook a further 6 mins at full power as above. Spoon out on to warm plates to serve.

MERMAID PIE

Like Shepherd's Pie but made with fish

Illustrated on page 36

CREAMED POTATOES
1½ lb/675 g old potatoes

5 tablespoons boiling water

½ oz/15 g butter or margarine

5 tablespoons milk

seasoning to taste

SAUCE
½ pt/275 ml milk taken from the refrigerator

1 oz/25 g butter or margarine

1 oz/25 g flour

2–3 oz/50–75 g grated cheese

1 level teaspoon prepared mustard

seasoning to taste

FISH
1 lb/450 g cod or haddock fillet at kitchen
    temperature

melted butter

paprika

salt and pepper

TO FINISH
1½ oz/40 g grated Red Leicester cheese

nutmeg or paprika

serves 4

1. Wash potatoes and slice thinly. Cut each medium potato into 8 chunks; large ones into 16.
2. Put into a 2 pt/1.25 litre glass or pottery dish with the water.
Cover with matching lid or cling film, puncturing the latter twice.
3. Cook 15 mins at full power, turning dish 4 times unless oven has a turntable. Leave to stand 3 mins, uncover and drain.
4. Mash potatoes finely. Add butter or margarine and seasoning, then beat in milk.
5. To make the sauce, pour milk into a glass or pottery jug. Leave uncovered and heat 1½ mins at full power until fairly hot. Remove from oven.
6. Put butter or margarine into a bowl. Leave uncovered and melt 1–1½ mins at defrost setting.
7. Stir in flour to form a roux and cook ½ min at full power. Remove from oven and gradually blend in the warm milk.

8. Return to oven and cook, uncovered, until sauce comes to the boil and thickens. Add grated cheese, mustard and seasoning. Allow 4 mins at full power, stirring every min.
9. To cook fish, arrange in a shallow dish and baste with melted butter or margarine. Add seasonings and cover with cling film punctured twice. Cook 5–6 mins at full power, turning dish twice unless oven has a turntable.
10. Remove any skin and bones and flake fish.
11. Put fish into a 3 pt/1.75 litre serving dish and stir in cheese sauce. Top with creamed potatoes.
12. Sprinkle lightly with grated cheese and either nutmeg or paprika. Leave uncovered and reheat for 6–7 mins at full power, turning dish 3 times unless oven has a turntable.
Serve with vegetables to taste.

SOUSED HERRINGS

4 herrings (each 1 lb/450 g) filleted

2 medium bay leaves, each broken into 4 pieces

6 oz/175 g onions, peeled and cut into thin
    slices

1 level tablespoon mixed pickling spice

¼ pt/150 ml boiling water

2 rounded teaspoons granulated sugar

2 level teaspoons salt

6 tablespoons wine or cider vinegar

serves 4

1. Roll up each fillet from head end to tail, skin side inside. Arrange around edge of a 10 in/25 cm round glass or pottery dish which is 2–3 ins/5–7.5 cm deep.
2. Stud here and there with bay leaves and onion slices separated into rings. Sprinkle with pickling spice.
3. Mix boiling water with sugar, salt and vinegar. Stir well then spoon over fish.
4. Cover with cling film, then puncture twice with the tip of a knife. Cook 18 mins at full power, turning 3 times unless oven has a turntable.
5. Cool, refrigerate until cold then uncover and serve.

VICTORIAN HASHED FISH

A nostalgic taste of the past, each helping of hash topped with an egg.

FISH

1½ lb/675 g fresh haddock or cod fillet, at kitchen temperature

melted butter or margarine

paprika

salt and pepper

2 oz/50 g butter or margarine

2 medium leeks, trimmed, slit then well-washed and sliced

12 oz/350 g cold cooked potatoes, diced

¼ pt/150 ml single cream

1 level teaspoon salt

4 eggs (size 3)

mild vinegar

serves 4

1. To cook fish, arrange in a shallow dish, brush with melted butter and dust with paprika and seasoning. Cover with cling film and puncture film twice with the point of a knife. Cook for about 8 mins until fish is creamy-looking and slightly flaky. Turn dish twice unless oven has a turntable. Remove any skin and bones and flake fish.
2. Put butter or margarine into an 8 in/ 20 cm round glass or pottery dish and melt 1½–2 mins at defrost setting. Leave uncovered.
3. Add leeks and mix in well. Cover with a plate and cook 5 mins at full power.
4. Stir in fish, potatoes, cream and salt. Cover as above and reheat until very hot, allowing 5–7 mins at full power. Stir once or twice. Keep warm.
5. Poach two eggs at a time, in individual small dishes. Put 6 tablespoons hot water into each glass or pottery dish and add ½ teaspoon mild vinegar to each to prevent the white from spreading. Carefully break an egg into each and puncture the yolks twice with the tip of a knife. Cover dishes with plates.
6. Cook two at a time for 1½–2 mins at full power, depending on how firm you like the whites. Leave to stand for 1¾ mins. Cook for an extra 15–20 secs if whites are too runny.
7. Remove egs with a perforated draining spoon. Put hash on to 4 warmed plates and top each with an egg.

MEDITERRANEAN TROUT

A lovely way to cook large, fleshy trout. Its ideal partners are baby new potatoes and French beans.

2 large trout (each 1½ lb/675 g) gutted and cleaned (heads left on)

4 tablespoons salad oil

4 tablespoons lemon juice

4 level tablespoons tomato purée

1 level teaspoon basil or oregano

1½ level teaspoons salt

3 level tablespoons drained capers

2 level tablespoons chopped parsley

serves 6

1. Wash and dry both fish. Arrange, head to tail, in an oblong dish of 10½ × 8 × 3 in (about 27 × 20 × 7.5 cm).
2. Beat all remaining ingredients well together and spoon over trout.
3. Cover dish with matching lid or cling film, puncturing the latter twice with the tip of a knife.
4. Cook 18 mins at full power, turning dish twice. Leave to stand 5 mins inside or outside the oven, whichever is the most convenient.
5. Uncover dish. To serve, carefully peel off skin then ease trout flesh away from centre bone.
6. Transfer to warm plates then coat with cooking juices.

Note *If liked, garnish each serving with a slice of lemon.*

*Mermaid Pie, served with carrots and
fresh beans*
Recipe on page 34

MAIN DISHES:
SOMETHING EXOTIC

CHICKEN WITH CHINESE GOLD SAUCE

Gently sweet-sour and delicately spiced, this Chinese-style chicken dish goes best with cooked bean sprouts and Chinese leaves.

SAFFRON RICE

8 oz/225 g easy-cook, long grain rice

1 pt/575 ml boiling water

1 level teaspoon salt

6–8 saffron strands

(the addition of a ¼ level teaspoon turmeric makes a more economic substitute for costly saffron)

2 lb/900 g chicken joints, washed and dried then dusted with plain flour

2 oz/50 g onion, peeled and grated

2 garlic cloves, peeled and crushed

2 tablespoons soy sauce

2 tablespoons medium sherry

2 tablespoons salad oil

4 tablespoons lemon juice

4 level tablespoons light brown soft sugar

2 slightly rounded tablespoons melted apricot jam minus large pieces of fruit

1 level teaspoon coriander

3 drops Tabasco

serves 4

1. Put rice into a fairly large glass or pottery dish. Add boiling water, saffron or turmeric and salt.
Stir round. Cover with cling film, then puncture twice with the tip of a knife.
Cook 16 mins at full power, turning dish 4 times unless oven has a turntable. Leave to stand 8 mins inside or outside oven, whichever is the most convenient, so that rice grains absorb all the liquid.
2. Arrange chicken joints in a fairly shallow, 10 in/25 cm round glass or pottery dish with skin sides facing. Slash through to flesh in several places with a sharp knife.
3. Beat rest of ingredients well together and pour over chicken. Cover loosely and leave to stand at kitchen temperature for 2 hours (1½ hours in the height of summer), turning over chicken joints 3 times.
4. Finally turn the chicken joints so that skin sides are again facing. Cover dish with cling film, then puncture twice with tip of a knife.
5. Cook 22 mins at full power, turning dish 4 times unless oven has a turntable. Serve, coated with pan juices on a bed of rice, first reheated 5–6 mins at defrost setting.

PINEAPPLE CHICKEN LOAF

Serve cold, cut into slices and accompany with salad vegetables

1 lb/450 g cold cooked chicken, finely minced

3 oz/75 g onions, peeled and finely minced

1 can crushed pineapple in syrup (about 1 lb/450 g in size with a drained weight of between 8–9 oz/225–250 g)

2 packets (each 26.5 g or just under the official ounce) bread sauce mix

¼ level teaspoon salt

2 eggs (size 3) beaten

1 oz/25 g flaked and toasted almonds (microwave 2–3 mins at full power)

serves 8 (F)

1. Line a 1½ pt/850 ml oblong, glass pie dish smoothly with cling film.
2. Put chicken and onions into a bowl. Fork in pineapple with its syrup, bread sauce mix, salt and eggs. Mix thoroughly.
3. Spread smoothly into prepared dish. Sprinkle with flaked almonds.
4. Leave uncovered and cook 30 mins at defrost setting, turning dish 3 or 4 times unless oven has a turntable.
5. Remove from oven. Lift out of dish when lukewarm and stand on a wire cooling rack. Peel away cling film when loaf is completely cold. Wrap leftovers and store in the refrigerator.

CHINESE-STYLE LETTUCE CHICKEN

A most delicious and authentically-flavoured chicken dish which should be served with freshly cooked noodles and any green vegetable to taste.

2¼ lb/just over 1 kg chicken wings
1 large lettuce (about 8 oz/225 g) washed, shaken dry and finely shredded
8 oz/225 g onions, peeled and very thinly sliced
1 oz/25 g fresh ginger, peeled and very thinly sliced
1 tablespoon salad oil
½ pt/275 ml boiling water
1½ level tablespoons cornflour
½ level teaspoon 5-star spice (5-spice powder)
4 tablespoons cold water
1 teaspoon soy sauce
1 level teaspoon salt

serves 4

1. Wash and dry chicken wings. Leave aside temporarily.
2. Put lettuce, onions, ginger and oil into an oblong dish measuring 10½ × 8 × 3 in/ 27 × 20 × 7.5 cm.
3. Cover with matching lid or cling film, puncturing the latter twice with the tip of a knife.
4. Cook 5 mins at full power. Uncover then add boiling water.
5. Put cornflour into a basin with spice. Blend smoothly with the cold water. Stir in soy sauce and salt. Stir into lettuce mixture.
6. Add chicken and mix in thoroughly. Cover again as above.
7. Cook 20 mins at full power, turning dish 4 times. Leave to stand 5 mins inside or outside the oven, whichever is the most convenient. Uncover, stir round and serve.

CHESTNUT CHICKEN

Most acceptable with brown rice and cooked peas, mixed together while hot with butter or margarine and a tablespoon of fresh coriander, finely chopped.

BROWN RICE
1 level teaspoon salt
4 oz/125 g brown rice
1¾ pt/1 litre boiling water

CHICKEN
2 oz/50 g butter or margarine
8 oz/225 g onions, peeled and finely chopped or grated
1 can (about 15 oz or 430 g) natural chestnut purée.
½ level teaspoon salt
4 chicken breasts (1 lb/450 g), washed and dried
8 oz/225 g blanched tomatoes, skinned and sliced
2 level tablespoons chopped parsley

serves generously (F)

1. To cook rice, put all ingredients into a 3½ pt/2 litre glass or pottery dish and stand on a plate in case water boils over.
2. Stir round to mix. Cover with cling film, then puncture twice with the tip of a knife. Alternatively, cover with matching lid.
3. Cook 35 mins at full power, turning 4 times unless oven has a turntable. Leave to stand 10 mins inside or outside the oven, whichever is the most convenient. Keep warm.
4. Put butter or margarine into a 10 in/25 cm round, shallow dish. Melt, uncovered, for 1½–2 mins at defrost setting.
5. Mix in onions and cook, also uncovered, for 4 mins at full power. Stir in chestnut purée smoothly then season with salt.
6. Flatten into an even layer and arrange chicken breasts on top round edge of dish. Top with tomato slices and sprinkle with parsley.
7. Cover with cling film, then puncture twice with the tip of a knife. Alternatively, cover with matching lid.
8. Cook 10 mins at full power, turning dish 4 times unless oven has a turntable.
9. Leave to stand 5 mins inside or outside the oven, whichever is the most convenient. Fluff up rice, spoon onto 4 warm serving plates and top with chicken.

CHICKEN AND VEGETABLE PAPRIKA CREAM

Provides a quietly subtle main course, delicately pink and perfect with small pastini.

PASTA

8 oz/225 g small pasta shells or bows

1½ pt/850 ml boiling water

1 level teaspoon salt

2 level teaspoons salad oil

1 oz/25 g butter or margarine, at kitchen temperature

8 oz/225 g onions, peeled and chopped

1 small green pepper (2 oz/50 g), washed and dried then de-seeded and chopped

6 oz/175 g washed and dried courgettes, very thinly sliced

12 oz/350 g chicken breast fillet, diced

1 level tablespoon paprika

3 level tablespoons tubed or canned tomato purée

1 carton (5 oz/142 ml) soured cream

1 level teaspoon salt

serves 4 (F)

1. To cook pasta, put into a large glass or pottery dish. Add water, salt and oil. Leave uncovered and cook 10 mins at full power, stirring gently 4 times.
Remove from oven, cover and keep warm.
2. Put butter or margarine in an 8 × 2 in/20 × 5 cm round dish and melt, uncovered, 1–1½ mins at defrost setting.
3. Stir in onions, leave uncovered and cook 3 mins at full power.
4. Mix in peppers courgettes, chicken breast, paprika and tomato purée. Cover with the cling film, then puncture twice with the tip of a knife. Alternatively, cover with a matching lid.
5. Cook 5 mins at full power, turning dish twice unless oven has a turntable.
Uncover. Mix in soured cream and salt thoroughly. Re-cover.
6. Cook a further 8 mins at full power, turning dish 4 times if oven has no turntable. Again stir round, adjust seasoning to taste.
7. Drain pasta and serve straight away with chicken.
A lettuce salad, tossed in a mild French dressing, makes a worthy accompaniment.

LAMB SPLITS

Divine with spiced aubergine purée and microwaved Pitta or sesame bread to mop up the juices

4 pieces of neck of lamb fillets, each 5–6 in/12.5–15 cm in length with total weight of 1½ lb/675 g

3 oz/75 g fresh white bread, cubed with crusts left on

3 oz/75 g onions, peeled and cut into biggish pieces

1 oz/25 g pine nuts, toasted under the grill or in microwave (2–3 mins at full power)

1 oz/25 g currants

½ level teaspoon salt

4 heaped teaspoons thick Greek yogurt

cinnamon

1½ oz/40 g button mushrooms, trimmed

½ oz/15 g butter or margarine, melted ¾ min at defrost setting

serves 4 (F)

1. Cut as much fat as possible off lamb fillets, then make a lengthwise slit in each, taking care not to cut right through or filling will fall out.
2. Turn bread into crumbs and very finely grate onions. If you have a food processor or blender, this will save effort.
3. Mix crumbs and onions with nuts, currants, and salt. Spoon equal amounts into lamb fillets.
4. Place round the edges of a 10 in/25 cm fairly shallow round dish to form a square. Smear tops of each with yogurt then sprinkle with a trace of cinnamon. Stud with mushrooms and coat with melted butter or margarine.
5. Cover with cling film, then puncture twice with the tip of a knife. Alternatively, cover with a matching lid.
6. Cook 14 mins at full power, turning dish 4 times unless oven has a turntable. Leave to stand 5 mins before serving.

EASTERN MINT KEBABS

When there is a high proportion of meat to metal and provided the metal has no direct contact with the sides of the cooker, metal skewers may be used for the Kebabs without upsetting the action of the microwave. Therefore tackle these Kebabs with confidence and serve them on Saffron Rice and with a Greek-style salad of mixed vegetables topped with pieces of Feta cheese, tiny black olives and a drizzle of olive oil.

RICE

8 oz/225 g easy-cook, long grain rice

1 pt/575 ml boiling water

*6–8 saffron strands or
    ½ level teaspoon turmeric*

1 level teaspoon salt

2 lb/900 g neck of lamb fillet

12 large fresh mint leaves (or use dried bay leaves, first microwaved in 4 tablespoons water for 2 mins at full power)

2 rounded tablespoons thick yogurt

3 rounded tablespoons tomato ketchup

1 garlic clove, peeled and crushed

1 teaspoon Worcestershire sauce

serves 6

1. Put rice into a fairly large glass or pottery dish. Add boiling water, saffron or turmeric and salt. Stir round. Cover with cling film, then puncture twice with the tip of a knife. Cook 16 mins at full power, turning dish 4 times unless oven has a turntable. Leave to stand 8 mins inside or outside the oven, so that rice grains absorb all the liquid. Keep warm.
2. Trim fat off lamb fillet then cut meat into 1 in/2.5 cm slices. Thread onto 6 skewers, each 4 ins/10 cm long, alternately with mint or softened bay leaves.
3. Arrange, like spokes of a wheel, in a 10 in/25 cm round shallow dish. For baste, beat yogurt with rest of ingredients. Brush about half over kebabs.
4. Cook, uncovered, for 7 mins at full power, turning dish twice unless oven has a turntable.

5. Remove from oven and turn Kebabs over. Brush with rest of baste. Cook a further 7 mins at full power, turning as before. Leave to stand 5 mins.
6. Uncover rice and fluff up with a fork, adding ½ oz/15 g butter or margarine if desired. Transfer to 6 warm plates and add a Kebab to each.

INDONESIAN-STYLE PEANUT AND COCONUT MINCE

Minced beef with a touch of originality is the theme of this main course, based on a Far Eastern idea. Serve with freshly cooked rice and a dish of mixed pickles.

6 oz/175 g onions, peeled and finely chopped

1 garlic clove, peeled and crushed

1 lb/450 g minced beef, as lean as possible

4 oz/125 g crunchy peanut butter

1 oz/25 g desiccated coconut

¼ teaspoon Tabasco

1 tablespoon soy sauce

½ level teaspoon salt

½ pt/275 ml boiling water

serves 4

1. Put onions, garlic and beef into a 2½ pt/ 1.5 litre dish. Mix well with a fork, taking particular care to break up the mince as finely as possible.
2. Cover with a matching lid or cling film, puncturing the latter twice with the tip of a knife. Cook 8 mins at full power, turning twice unless oven has a turntable.
3. Uncover then stir in all remaining ingredients. When thoroughly mixed, cover again as above.
4. Cook 8 mins at full power, turning dish 3 times. Uncover, stir round and serve.

Curried Mushrooms with Bulgar, served
with a salad of chopped tomatoes and
cucumber,
yogurt mixed with mint.
Recipe on page 43

BLUE CHEESE AND WALNUT FLAN

Serve with a crunchy chicory and orange salad, tossed in a zesty French dressing and spinkled here and there with watercress leaves.

PASTRY

6 oz/175 g plain flour

pinch of salt

3 oz/75 g butter or margarine, at kitchen temperature

1 oz/25 g walnuts, finely chopped

about 7 teaspoons cold water to mix

1 egg yolk from size 3 egg

FILLING

1 packet (7 oz/200 g) full fat cream cheese, at kitchen temperature

2 level tablespoons snipped fresh chives or the light green part of very well-washed leek, finely chopped

4 oz/125 g soft blue cheese such as Lymeswold or Gorgonzola, at kitchen temperature

1 level teaspoon paprika

2 eggs (size 3) at kitchen temperature and well-beaten

4 tablespoons milk.

serves 4

1. For pastry, sift flour and salt into a bowl. Rub in fat finely, toss in walnuts then mix to a stiff paste with cold water.
2. Turn out on to a floured surface, knead lightly until smooth then roll out fairly thinly into a circle. Use to line a lightly greased 8 in/20 cm glass or pottery pie plate. Pinch top edge into flutes between finger and thumb then prick all over with a fork. Cook 6 mins, uncovered, at full power, turning 4 times unless oven has a turntable. If pastry has bulged in places, press down very gently with fingers protected by oven gloves.
3. Remove from oven and brush all over with egg yolk. Cook a further min at full power to seal holes. Leave to stand while preparing filling.
4. Beat cream cheese until light and very soft. Add chives. Mash in blue cheese then add rest of ingredients. Beat well until completely smooth. Pour into pastry case. Cook, uncovered, 14 mins at defrost setting, turning 4 times unless oven has a turntable. Serve warm or cold, cut into wedges.

PROVENCALE PRAWNS

RICE

8 oz/225 g easy-cook, long-grain rice

1 pt/575 ml boiling water

1 level teaspoon salt

1 oz/25 g butter or margarine (or 1 tablespoon olive oil, if preferred)

2 oz/50 g onion, peeled and grated

1 garlic clove, peeled and crushed

1 can (14 oz/400 g) tomatoes, drained

1 level teaspoon Italian seasoning or dried basil

1 level teaspoon dark brown soft sugar

1 lb/450 g frozen peeled prawns, used from frozen

seasoning to taste

chopped parsley

serves 4 to 6

1. Put rice into a fairly large glass or pottery dish. Add boiling water and salt. Stir round to mix. Cover with cling film, then puncture twice with the tip of a knife.
Cook 16 mins at full power, turning dish 4 times unless oven has a turntable.
Leave to stand 8 mins so that rice grains absorb all the liquid.
2. Put butter, margarine or oil into a 3 pt/1.75 litre glass or pottery serving dish and heat 1½ mins at defrost setting. Leave uncovered.
3. Stir in onion and garlic. Leave uncovered and cook 3 mins at full power. Stir round.
4. Add tomatoes, Italian seasoning or basil and sugar. Cover with a plate and cook 5 mins at full power, stirring twice.
5. Add prawns and cover as above. Cook 4 mins then carefully separate. Re-cover and cook a further 3 to 4 mins. Adjust seasoning to taste and sprinkle with parsley.
6. Reheat rice 5–6 mins at defrost setting. Fork in about 1 rounded tablespoon chopped parsley and ½ oz/15 g butter or margarine if desired. Arrange on hot plates then top with prawns.

MAIN DISHES:
SOMETHING VEGETARIAN

TOMATO UPSIDE-DOWN CHEESE PUDDING

Serve with a green vegetable

8 oz/225 g self-raising flour

1 level teaspoon powdered mustard

½ level teaspoon salt

4 oz/125 g butter or margarine

4 oz/125 g Cheddar cheese, finely grated

2 eggs (size 3) beaten

¼ pt/150 ml cold milk

1 lb/450 g tomatoes, blanched and skinned

½ level teaspoon salt

1 rounded tablespoon chopped parsley

serves 4

1. Well-grease a 3 pt/1.75 litre deep round dish.
2. Sift flour, mustard and salt into a bowl. Rub in butter or margarine finely. Toss in cheese.
3. Using a fork, mix to a soft consistency with eggs and milk. Spoon into dish and spread evenly with a knife.
4. Cook, uncovered, for 6 mins at full power, turning dish 4 times unless oven has a turntable.
5. Meanwhile skin tomatoes and chop. Mix with salt. Put into a shallow bowl and cover with a plate.
6. Remove pudding from oven and invert into a dish. Return to oven and cook a further 2 mins at full power.
7. Remove from oven, cover with kitchen paper and leave aside temporarily. Heat tomatoes for 3 mins at full power. Spoon over pudding, sprinkle with parsley and serve while still hot.

CURRIED MUSHROOMS WITH BULGAR

Accompany with side dishes of chutney, sliced hardboiled eggs showered with chopped walnuts, yogurt mixed with 1 or 2 teaspoons chopped mint, and a salad of chopped tomatoes and cucumber.

Illustrated on page 41

BULGAR
8 oz/225 g bulgar

1 pt/575 ml boiling water

1–1½ level teaspoons salt

CURRIED MUSHROOMS
2 lb/900 g button mushrooms

2 oz/50 g butter or margarine

1 level tablespoon curry powder

1 level teaspoon salt

¼ pt/150 ml buttermilk

1 level teaspoon caster sugar

¼ level teaspoon garlic powder

1 level tablespoon cornflour

2 tablespoons cold water

serves 6

1. Put bulgar into an 8 in/20 cm round and fairly deep glass or pottery dish. Leave uncovered and toast, with no water, for 3 mins at full power, stirring at the end of every min.
2. Mix in boiling water. Cook, uncovered, for 5 mins at full power, stirring 3 times. Season to taste, cover and keep hot.
3. Trim mushrooms then wash and dry. Leave aside temporarily.
4. Put butter or margarine into a 4 pt/2.25 litre glass or pottery dish and melt 1½–2 mins at defrost setting. Leave uncovered.
5. Add curry powder, salt, buttermilk, caster sugar and garlic powder. Cover with a plate and cook 2 mins at full power.
6. Toss in mushrooms. Add cornflour, smoothly mixed with water. Cover as above and cook 7 mins at full power, stirring twice.
7. Uncover, stir again and serve over portions of bulgar.

*Leek and Chestnut Casserole, served
with jacket potatoes*

LENTIL AND BULGAR CASSEROLE

*Ready in under 15 mins, this healthy mix of ingredients
makes for a nutritious and wholesome companion when it
comes to egg, fish and cheese dishes. Also, it is based on
store cupboard ingredients, so is ideal for unexpected callers.*

8 oz/225 g bulgar
6 oz/175 g orange lentils
2 pt/1.2 litre boiling water
2 slightly rounded tablespoons dried chopped red and green pepper flakes
1 slightly rounded tablespoon dried chopped parsley
1 level teaspoon onion salt
½ level teaspoon salt

serves 6 to 8

1. Put all ingredients into a 4 pt/2.25 litre
casserole with lid. Stir round and cover.
2. Cook for 14 mins at full power, turning
dish 3 times unless oven has a turntable. Stir
twice with a fork.
3. Leave to stand 5 mins inside or outside
the oven, whichever is the most convenient.
Serve as desired.
*Note Leftovers may be tossed with French dressing and
served cold as a salad.*

LEEK AND CHESTNUT CASSEROLE

Serve with microwaved jacket potatoes and tomatoes.

8 oz/225 g dried chestnuts
2 large leeks
1 oz/25 g butter or margarine
½ to 1 level teaspoon salt

serves 4 (F)

1. To cook Chestnuts: wash thoroughly. Put
into a 3 pt/1.75 litre dish and mix in 1 pt/
575 ml boiling water. Cover with a plate and
cook 15 mins at full power. Leave to stand
14 mins inside or outside the oven,
whichever is the most convenient. Cook a
further 15 mins at full power then stand for
another 15 mins. Add an extra ¼ pt/150 ml
boiling water and cook a further 10 mins at
full power. Remove from oven and stir

round. Cover again with a plate and leave to
stand for a final ¼ hour.
2. Trim leeks, leaving on 2 in/5 cm of green
'skirt'. Slit and wash very thoroughly to
remove earth and grit, then cut into ½ in/
1.25 cm slices.
3. Put butter or margarine into a 7 in/
17.5 cm round glass or pottery casserole and
melt 1–1½ mins at defrost setting.
4. Mix in leeks, cover with a plate and cook
for 6 mins at full power, stirring twice.
5. Break up chestnuts and combine with
leeks. Sprinkle with salt. Cover as above and
cook a further 3 mins at full power. Stir and
serve.

PINE NUT AND RAISIN COUSCOUS

*With the couscous lightly toasted in the microwave, this
makes a most unusual accompaniment for poultry, egg and
fish dishes. It can also be eaten on its own with salad.*

1 oz/25 g pine nuts
2 tablespoons salad oil
8 oz/225 g packeted couscous
2 oz/50 g raisins
1 level teaspoon salt
1 pt/575 ml boiling water

serves 6

1. Put all the ingredients into a 3 pt/1.75
litre casserole dish with lid. Stir round and
cover.
2. Cook 4½ mins at full power, stirring twice.
3. Leave to stand 5 mins inside or outside
the microwave, whichever is the most
convenient.
4. Stir round again, using a fork. Serve as
desired.

WAY DOWN YONDER AUBERGINE CASSEROLE

Can be 'hotted-up' by the addition of a few drops of Tabasco after the salt

AUBERGINES

1 lb/450 g aubergines, peeled and cut into 2 in/5 cm pieces

4 tablespoons boiling water

1 oz/25 g butter or margarine

2 oz/50 g celery, scrubbed and finely chopped

6 oz/175 g onions, peeled and finely chopped

2 oz/50 g red or green pepper, de-seeded and finely chopped

6 oz/175 g blanched tomatoes, skinned and chopped

3 oz/75 g fresh white breadcrumbs

½–1 level teaspoon salt

2 oz/50 g Double Gloucester cheese, grated

serves 4

1. To cook the aubergines, tip into a basin and add the water. Cover with cling film, then puncture twice with the tip of a knife. Alternatively, cover with a matching lid.
2. Cook for 6 mins at full power, turning dish twice unless oven has a turntable. Remove from oven, stand 2 mins and drain.
3. Transfer aubergines to a blender goblet or food processor. Run machine until mixture forms a smooth purée.
4. Heat butter or margarine, in a 2 pt/1.25 litre dish, for 1 min at full power. Leave uncovered.
5. Stir in celery, onions and pepper. Cover with plate or matching lid and cook 3 mins at full power. Mix in aubergine purée, tomatoes, crumbs and salt.
6. Cover with plate or lid as above and cook another 3 mins at full power, turning dish twice unless oven has a turntable.
7. Uncover, sprinkle with cheese and cook 2 mins at full power, turning once. Stand 2–3 mins and serve.

VEGETARIAN STUFFED AUBERGINES

May be served hot or cold and team especially well with jacket potatoes and salad

Illustrated on page 48

2 medium aubergines (about 1¼ lb/575 g)

2 teaspoons lemon juice

3 oz/75 g fresh brown breadcrumbs

1 oz/25 g toasted pine nuts (Microwave 2–3 mins at full power)

1½ level teaspoons salt

1 level teaspoon garlic or onion powder

3 hardboiled eggs, chopped

4 tablespoons mixed herbs

4 teaspoons salad oil

serves 4

1. Slit skin of aubergines all the way round with a sharp knife, as though you were going to cut each aubergine in half lengthwise.
2. Put on to a plate, cover with a piece of kitchen paper and cook 6 mins at full power when aubergines should be tender.
3. Remove from oven and cut each in half along split lines. Spoon pulp into blender or food processor. Add lemon juice. Run machine until mixture is smooth and purée-like.
4. Scrape into a bowl. Mix in crumbs, nuts, salt, garlic or onion powder, chopped eggs, milk and herbs.
5. Return to aubergine halves then stand on a plate, narrow ends towards centre. Trickle oil over tops, cover with kitchen paper and reheat 4 mins at full power.

MAIN DISHES:
SOMETHING TRADITIONAL

BEEF IN WINE WITH SAVOYARD POTATOES

For sheer luxury, accompany with cauliflower, coated with Hollandaise sauce

SAVOYARD-POTATOES

2 lb/900 g potatoes, peeled and cut into wafer thin slices

1 garlic clove, peeled and crushed, mixed with 3 oz/75 g butter or margarine, melted

6 oz/175 g grated cheese – Gruyère or Emmental are ideal but for greater economy, use Cheddar or Edam

1 level teaspoon salt

pepper to taste

½ pt/275 ml chicken stock, made with cube and water or white wine

paprika

BEEF IN WINE

8 oz/225 g onions, peeled

1 garlic clove, peeled (optional)

4 oz/125 g cup mushrooms, trimmed and outsides peeled

1 oz/25 g butter or margarine, at kitchen temperature

1 lb/450 g rump steak, cut into ½ inch/1.25 cm cubes

1 level tablespoon tubed or canned tomato purée

1 rounded tablespoon parsley

1 level tablespoon cornflour

1 level teaspoon prepared English or French mustard

½ pt/275 ml dry red wine

1 level teaspoon salt

serves 6 (F)

1. Grease a 10 in/25 cm round glass or pottery dish, of about 2 ins/5 cm in depth, with butter or margarine.
2. Fill with alternate layers of potatoes, two-thirds of the garlic and butter or margarine mixture, and the same amount of cheese. Begin and end with potatoes and sprinkle salt and pepper between layers.
3. Gently pour stock or wine down side of dish. Trickle rest of butter over the top then sprinkle with remaining cheese. Add a light dusting of paprika.
4. Cover with cling film, then puncture twice with the tip of a knife. Alternatively, cover with a matching lid.
5. Cook for 20 mins at full power, turning dish 4 times unless oven has a turntable. Leave to stand and keep warm.
6. Finely chop onions and garlic. Thinly slice mushrooms. Put butter or margarine in a round glass or pottery dish measuring about 8 × 2 in/20 × 5 cm. Heat, covered, for 1 min at full power.
7. Stir in prepared vegetables, leave uncovered and cook 5 mins at full power. Stir in steak then move mixture to edges of dish to form a ring with a hollow in the centre.
8. Cover with a plate and cook 5 mins at full power. Meanwhile mix together purée, parsley, cornflour and mustard. Blend in the wine. Pour gently into dish over steak and vegetables. Stir well to mix.
9. Cover with cling film, then puncture twice with the tip of a knife. Alternatively, cover with matching lid.
10. Cook beef 5 mins at full power, turning dish twice unless oven has a turntable. Leave to stand 5 mins inside or outside the oven, whichever is the most convenient. Season with salt. Serve hot with the Savoyard Potatoes.

Preparation of Vegetarian Stuffed Aubergines
Recipe on page 46

CURRIED MINCE WITH RICE

Fairly gentle and therefore safe for children. It goes best with curried lentils.

RICE

8 oz/225 g easy-cook, long-grain rice

1 pt/575 ml boiling water

1 level teaspoon salt

8 oz/225 g onions, peeled and chopped

1 lb/450 g lean minced beef

1 rounded tablespoon plain flour

1 level tablespoon mild curry powder

2 level tablespoons chutney (I used mango but use any other to suit)

1 level tablespoon tomato purée

½ pt/275 ml boiling water

1 brown gravy cube

salt and pepper to taste

serves 4 (F)

1. Put rice into a fairly large glass or pottery dish. Add boiling water and salt. Stir round to mix. Cover with cling film, then puncture twice with the tip of a knife.
Cook 16 mins at full power, turning dish 4 times unless oven has a turn table.
Leave to stand 8 mins so that rice grains absorb all the liquid.
2. Put onions and meat into an 8 × 2 in/ 20 × 5 cm round glass or pottery dish and mash well together.
3. Form into a ring round edge of dish. Cover with a plate and cook 5 mins at full power.
4. Remove from oven and mix in flour, curry powder, chutney, tomato purée and boiling water. Crumble in gravy cube. Season.
5. Cover with cling film, then puncture twice with the tip of a knife. Alternatively, cover with matching lid.
6. Cook 15 mins at full power, turning dish 4 times unless oven has a turntable. Leave to stand 5 mins, stir round and serve on a bed of rice, first reheated for about 6 mins at defrost setting.

BEEF IN STROGANOV MOOD

BROWN RICE

1 level teaspoon salt

4 oz/125 g brown rice

1¾ pt/1 litre boiling water

1 oz/25 g butter

3 oz/75 g onions, peeled

1 lb/450 g rump steak

4 oz/125 g button mushrooms

1 oz/25 g chopped gherkins

1 carton (5 oz or 142 ml) soured cream, at kitchen temperature

salt and pepper to taste

serves 6

1. To cook rice, put all ingredients into a 3½ pt/2 litre glass or pottery dish and stand on a plate in case water boils over.
2. Stir round to mix. Cover with cling film, then puncture twice with the tip of a knife. Alternatively, cover with matching lid.
3. Cook 35 mins at full power, turning 4 times unless oven has a turntable. Leave to stand 10 mins inside or outside the oven. Keep warm.
4. Put butter into an 8 × 2 inch 20 × 5 cm round dish. Cover and heat for 1 min at full power.
5. Grate onions. Cut steak into narrow strips against the grain. Very thinly slice mushrooms.
6. Add onions and steak to butter. Cover with a plate. Cook 4 mins at full power, turning dish twice unless oven has a turntable.
7. Stir in mushrooms and re-cover with the plate. Cook a further 2 mins, turning once. Mix in gherkins, cream and seasoning to taste. Cook, uncovered, for 1 more min at full power. Serve with the rice.

AUBERGINE MOUSSAKA

AUBERGINES

1½ lb/675 g aubergines, washed and dried

5 tablespoons boiling water

2 teaspoons lemon juice

FILLING

2 oz/50 g butter or margarine

8 oz/225 g onions, peeled and grated

12 oz/350 g cold cooked lamb or beef, minced

4 oz/125 g fresh white breadcrumbs

1 lb/450 g blanched tomatoes, skinned and chopped

1–1½ level teaspoon salt

SAUCE

¾ pt/425 ml milk

1½ oz/40 g butter or margarine

1½ oz/40 g plain flour

3 oz/75 g Cheddar cheese, grated

salt and pepper to taste

serves 8 (F)

1. Cut stems off aubergines and discard. Slice fairly thinly and put into a large dish. Add water mixed with lemon juice.
2. Cover with cling film, then puncture twice with the tip of a knife. Cook 12 mins at full power then leave to stand outside the oven for 15 mins.
3. Prepare filling. Put butter or margarine into a dish and melt about 1¾ mins at defrost setting. Mix in onions and cover with a plate. Cook 2 mins at full power. Mix in rest of ingredients.
4. Drain aubergines thoroughly and slice. Fill a 4 pt/2.25 litre greased dish with alternate layers of aubergine slices and meat mixture.
5. For sauce, heat milk in a Jug for 3½–4 mins or until hot but not boiling. Keep covered.
6. Melt butter or margarine, at defrost setting, for about 1¾ mins in a fairly large basin. Stir in flour then gradually whisk in milk.
7. Return to microwave and cook 2½–3 mins or until boiling, whisking gently at the end of every min. Stir in cheese, season to taste and pour over Moussaka.
8. Cover with cling film, slit twice and reheat at full power for 12–14 mins. Turn 3 or 4 times unless oven has a turntable. Stand 8 mins before serving.

TURKEY WITH ORANGE CRANBERRY SAUCE

SAUCE

4 oz/125 g cranberries, thawed if frozen

3½ tablespoons water

3 oz/75 g caster sugar

½ level teaspoon finely grated lemon peel

finely grated peel of ½ orange, washed and dried

BASTE

1 oz/25 g butter or margarine at kitchen temperature

2 rounded teaspoons tomato ketchup

1 level teaspoon paprika

1 teaspoon Worcestershire sauce

Whole turkey breast (bought ready prepared, on the bone) about 2–2¼ lb/1 kg, defrosted if frozen

serves 3

1. To make sauce, put all ingredients into a glass or pottery dish. Cover with a plate.
2. Cook 6 mins at full power, stirring sauce twice and crushing fruit against sides of bowl as you do so.
3. Remove from oven, keep covered and leave to cool.
4. To make baste, melt butter or margarine, uncovered, for 1–1½ mins at defrost setting. Stir in rest of ingredients.
5. Put turkey onto a plate, skin side uppermost. Brush with baste.
6. Cover with cling film, then puncture twice with the tip of a knife.
Cook at full power for 15–17 mins. Stand for 7 mins.
Serve with the Orange Cranberry Sauce.

CHICKEN BOURGUIGNONNE

More customarily made with beef, chicken is a distinguished substitute and produces a dish worthy of any gourmet.

Illustrated on page 53

1 oz/25 g butter or margarine

6 oz/175 g onions, peeled and chopped

1 garlic clove, peeled and crushed

6 chicken breast fillets (1½ lb/675 g), washed and dried

1 oz/25 g cornflour

1 level teaspoon prepared continental mustard

½ level teaspoon mixed herbs

½ pt/275 ml red burgundy

8 oz/225 g washed and dried mushrooms, thinly sliced

1 heaped tablespoon chopped parsley

serves 6

1. Put butter or margarine into a fairly shallow dish of about 10 × 8 in/25 × 20 cm. Leave uncovered and melt for 1½ mins at defrost setting.
2. Add onions and garlic. Cover dish with matching lid or cling film, puncturing the latter twice with the tip of a knife. Cook for 3 mins at full power. Uncover. Stir round.
3. Top with a single layer of chicken breasts. Cover as before and cook for 8 mins at full power. Uncover.
4. Tip cornflour into a basin then add mustard and herbs. Mix smoothly with 4 tablespoons of burgundy then blend in remainder.
5. Spoon over chicken. Sprinkle with mushrooms and parsley. Again cover as above and cook for 8 mins at full power, turning dish twice unless oven has a turntable.
6. Leave stand 3 mins inside or outside the oven, whichever is the most convenient. Uncover and serve with boiled potatoes and seasonal fresh vegetables.

LUXURY LAMB 'HOT POT'

1½ lb/675 g potatoes, peeled and washed

8 oz/225 g onions, peeled and washed

4 oz/125 g carrots, peeled and washed

4 oz/125 g celery, well-scrubbed

8 best end neck of lamb chops (about 2–2¼ lb/ 1 kg), surplus fat trimmed off

1 brown gravy cube

½ pt/275 ml boiling water

1 level teaspoon salt

½ oz/15 g butter or margarine, melted

serves 4 (F)

1. Very thinly slice potatoes, onions and carrots by hand or in a food processor. Thinly slice celery.
2. Arrange half the prepared vegetables, in layers, in a 4 pt/about 2.25 litre lightly greased casserole. Top with chops. Add remaining vegetables, again in layers, ending with potatoes.
3. Cover with cling film, then puncture twice with the tip of a knife. Alternatively, cover with matching lid. Cook 15 mins at full power, turning dish 4 times unless oven has a turntable.
4. Remove from oven and uncover. Crumble gravy cube into water then add salt. Pour gently down side of casserole. Drizzle butter or margarine over the top then cover as before.
5. Cook another 15 mins at full power, turning dish as before. Leave to stand 10 mins inside or outside the oven, whichever is the most convenient. Spoon out of dish and serve.

Sole Veronique, garnished with grapes

SOLE VERONIQUE

BÉCHAMEL SAUCE
$\frac{1}{2}$ pt/275 ml milk

bouquet garni

1 bay leaf

1 small peeled and quartered onion

2 sprigs of parsley

1 oz/25 g butter or margarine

1 oz/25 g plain flour

2 soles, each 12 oz/350 g

*3 oz/75 g green grapes, peeled, halved and de-
   seeded*

serves 2

1. To make sauce; pour milk into a glass or pottery jug. Add next 4 ingredients. Cover with saucer and bring just up to the boil; 5–6 mins at defrost setting. Strain.
2. Put butter or margarine into a bowl. Leave uncovered and heat 1–1$\frac{1}{2}$ mins at defrost setting.
3. Stir in flour to form a roux and cook $\frac{1}{2}$ min at full power. Remove from oven and gradually blend in milk. Return to oven and cook, uncovered, until sauce comes to boil and thickens. Allow 3–4 mins at full power and beat at end of every min.
4. Cook each fish individually.
Wash and wipe dry. Put into a shallow oblong glass or pottery dish.
Add 1 tablespoon hot water. Cover with cling film, then puncture twice with the tip of a knife.

Cook 4 mins at full power, turning once unless oven has a turntable. Leave to stand 2 mins. Continue to cook 5½–6 mins, turning twice.

5. Using 2 spatulas, lift sole on to a warm plate. Repeat with rest of fish. Coat with Béchamel sauce and garnish with grapes.

Chicken Bourguignonne, served with boiled potatoes and mange tout
Recipe on page 51

GAMMON WITH MUSTARD SAUCE

Piece of gammon, (about 3 lb/1.35 kg)

Demarara sugar

MUSTARD SAUCE
1 pt/575 ml milk, taken from the refrigerator

2 oz/50 g butter or margarine

2 oz/50 g plain flour

4 level teaspoons prepared English mustard

4 teaspoons lemon juice

seasoning to taste

serves 8

1. Boil gammon conventionally in 2 or 3 changes of water to reduce saltiness. Cool. Wrap narrow end (unless middle cut) in a piece of foil. Put into a large roasting bag and close top with an elastic band.
2. Microwave 12 mins at full power. Stand for 15 mins and then turn over. Continue to cook for another 12 mins. Leave to stand 15 more mins.
3. Carefully take out of bag and remove foil if used. Strip off skin then press sugar against fat for decoration.
4. Pour milk into a glass or pottery jug. Leave uncovered and heat 1½ mins at full power until fairly hot. Remove from oven.
5. Put butter or margarine into a bowl. Leave uncovered and melt 1–1½ mins at defrost setting.
6. Stir in flour to form a roux and cook ½ min at full power. Remove from oven and gradually blend in the warm milk.
7. Return to oven and cook, uncovered, until sauce comes to the boil and thickens. Allow about 3–4 mins at full power and beat at the end of every min to ensure sauce stays smooth.
8. Add mustard and lemon juice, season to taste, stir well and serve over slices of gammon.

FLAN ARNOLD BENNETT

Best accompanied by a crackling salad of firm lettuce, celery, cucumber, grated carrot and some coarsely chopped toasted hazelnuts tossed together with a piquant French dressing.

shortcrust pastry, made with 6 oz/175 g flour and 3 oz/75 g fat etc

1 egg yolk

4 oz/125 g cooked and flaked smoked haddock or cod fillet

3 eggs (size 2)

1 carton (5 oz/142 ml) soured cream

¼–½ level teaspoon salt

1 rounded tablespoon mayonnaise

3 oz/75 g Cheshire or Red Leicester cheese, grated

serves 6

1. Roll out pastry and use to line an 8 in/20 cm fluted flan dish. Prick well all over, especially where sides join the base.
2. Cook for 6 mins at full power, turning twice unless oven has a turntable. If pastry has bulged in places, press down very gently with fingers protected by oven gloves.
3. Brush all over with egg yolk then cook a further 1 min at full power to seal holes. Remove from oven and cover base with the fish.
4. Beat eggs well together with cream, salt and mayonnaise. Pour evenly over fish. Sprinkle with cheese and cook, uncovered, for 8 mins at full power, turning dish 4 times unless oven has a turntable. Serve warm or cold.

SKATE WITH CAPER SAUCE

SAUCE

$\frac{1}{2}$ pt/275 ml milk, taken from refrigerator

1 oz/25 g butter or margarine

1 oz/25 g plain flour

1 rounded tablespoon drained and chopped
  capers

seasoning to taste

Allow 6–8 oz/175–225 g skate per person, at
  kitchen temperature

melted butter or margarine

paprika

salt and pepper

1. Pour milk into a glass or pottery jug.
Leave uncovered and heat 1½ mins at full
power. Remove from oven.
2. Put butter or margarine into a bowl.
Leave uncovered and melt 1–1½ mins at
defrost setting.
3. Stir in flour to form a roux and cook ½
min at full power. Remove from oven and
gradually blend in the warm milk.
4. Return to the oven and cook, uncovered,
until sauce comes to the boil and thickens.
Stir in capers. Allow about 3–4 mins at full
power and beat at the end of every min to
ensure sauce stays smooth. Season to taste
and keep warm.
5. Arrange two portions of fish in a shallow
dish. Brush with melted butter and dust with
seasoning. Cover with cling film, then
puncture twice with the tip of a knife. Cook
for 5–6 mins per lb/450 g. Time will vary
according to thickness of fish so watch
carefully. Fish is ready when it is creamy-
looking and slightly flaky.
6. Serve with a coating of Caper Sauce.

TROUT WITH ALMONDS
Accompany with a mixed salad or spinach

2 oz/50 g butter

1 tablespoon fresh lemon juice

4 trout, each weighing 6 to 8 oz/175–225 g,
  cleaned and well-washed

2 oz/50 g flaked and toasted almonds
  (microwave 5 mins at full power)

salt and pepper to taste

GARNISH
4 lemon wedges

parsley sprigs

serves 4

1. Put butter into a small dish and melt for
1½–2 mins at defrost setting. Stir in lemon
juice.
2. Arrange trout, head to tail, in a buttered
dish measuring about 10 × 8 in/25 × 20 cm.
Remove turntable if necessary, or place
turntable upside down, if model permits, to
prevent it from rotating. This will stop the
dish banging against the side of the oven and
causing damage.
3. Coat with melted butter and lemon juice
then sprinkle with almonds and seasoning.
4. Cover with cling film, then puncture
twice with the tip of a knife.
5. Cook 9–12 mins, turning dish twice.
Leave to stand 5 mins then transfer to 4
warm plates.
6. Coat with juices from dish and garnish
with lemon wedges and parsley.

Preparation of Eastern Gold Rice

SWEETCORN AND CHICKEN RICE

8 oz/225 g easy-cook, long grain rice
1 pt/575 ml boiling water
1 level teaspoon salt
4 oz/125 g frozen sweetcorn
2 oz/50 g chopped-up red pepper
6 oz/175 g cut-up cooked chicken

serves 3–4 (F)

1. Put rice into a fairly large glass or pottery dish. Add boiling water and salt and remaining ingredients. Stir round to mix. Cover with cling film, then puncture twice with the tip of a knife. Cook 18 mins at full power, turning dish 4 times unless oven has a turntable.
2. Leave to stand 8–9 mins so that rice grains absorb all the liquid. Remove film, fluff up with a fork, adding ½–1 oz/15–25 g butter or margarine if desired.
Sprinkle with paprika before serving.

EASTERN GOLD RICE

A lovely accompaniment to kebabs or lamb roasts

2 oz/50 g dried apricots
hot water
1 oz/25 g pine nuts
8 oz/225 g easy-cook, long grain rice
1 chicken stock cube
1 pt/575 ml boiling water
1 level teaspoon salt
½ level teaspoon saffron strands, crushed in a mortar with pestle

serves 6 (F)

1. Wash apricots thoroughly and put into a cup. Add hot water to cover. Top with a saucer. Microwave for 2 mins at full power. Drain. Snip into small pieces with scissors.
2. Toast pine nuts under the grill until deep gold, or microwave for 2–3 mins at full power and leave until cold and crisp.
3. Tip rice into a deep dish. Crumble over stock cube then mix in water, salt and saffron. Add prepared apricots and nuts.
4. Stir round. Cover with cling film, then puncture twice with the tip of a knife. Alternatively, cover with matching lid.
5. Cook for 15 mins at full power, turning dish 4 times unless oven has a turntable.
6. Uncover then fluff up with a fork. Serve hot.

CURRIED KEDGEREE

12 oz/350 g smoked haddock fillet
4 tablespoons cold water
2 oz/50 g butter or margarine
8 oz/225 g easy-cook, long grain rice
1 level tablespoon to taste, mild curry powder
1 pt/575 ml boiling water
3 hardboiled eggs (size 3) shelled and 2 chopped
¼ pt/150 ml single cream
seasoning to taste
chopped parsley for garnishing

serves 4

1. Put fish into a shallow glass or pottery dish and add the cold water. Cover with cling film, then puncture twice with the tip of a knife.
2. Cook 5 mins at full power, turning dish once. Drain fish and flake up flesh with 2 forks, discarding skin and bones.
3. Put butter or margarine in a 3 pt/1.75 litre glass or pottery dish and melt, uncovered, 1½–2 mins at defrost setting. Stir in rice, curry powder and boiling water.
4. Cover with film as above and cook 15 mins at full power, turning dish 3 times unless oven has a turntable. Uncover then stir in flaked fish, 2 chopped eggs and the cream. Season to taste.
5. Fluff up with a fork, cover with a plate and reheat 5 mins at full power. Remove from oven then garnish with the third egg, first cut into slices or wedges. Add a heavy dusting of the parsley. Serve, as desired, with chutney.

FAMILY PASTA POT

A useful dish if you happen to have leftover meat to use up.
Serve with Brussels sprouts and carrots, or even cooked red
cabbage for novelty.

Illustrated on page 60

1 oz/25 g butter or margarine, at kitchen temperature
6 oz/175 g onions, peeled and chopped
8 oz/225 g pasta bows or shells (uncooked)
8 oz/225 g tomatoes, blanched and skinned then chopped
12 oz/350 g boiled bacon, gammon or cold cooked sausages, cubed
1¼ pt/725 ml hot stock, made with cubes and water
1 level teaspoon salt
1 level teaspoon mixed herbs
1 level tablespoon tubed or canned tomato purée

serves 4 generously

1. Put butter or margarine into a 3–3½ pt/
1.75–2 litre round glass or pottery dish.
Leave uncovered and melt for 1–1½ mins at
defrost setting. Stir in onions. Continue to
cook, still uncovered, for 2 mins at full
power.
2. Mix in pasta bows or shells and tomatoes
then add either the bacon, gammon or cold
cooked sausages.
3. Combine stock with rest of ingredients,
pour into dish of pasta and mix well. Cover
with cling film, then puncture twice with the
tip of a knife. Alternatively, cover with a
matching lid.
4. Cook 25 mins at full power, turning dish
4 times unless oven has a turntable. Leave to
stand 5 mins inside or outside the oven,
whichever is the most convenient.
5. Uncover. Stir round and serve with
accompaniments as suggested above.

PAELLA CHICKEN

1 oz/25 g butter or margarine
4 oz/125 g streaky bacon, chopped
1 garlic clove, peeled and crushed
8 oz/225 g onions, peeled and very finely chopped
1 can (about 6¼ oz/185 g) red pimientos, drained and fairly finely chopped
1 can (14 oz/400 g) tomatoes
8 oz/225 g easy-cook, long grain rice
1 level teaspoon paprika
2 rounded teaspoons turmeric
6 oz/175 g frozen peas
2 lb/900 g chicken joints, thawed if frozen
soy sauce
4 oz/125 g peeled, cooked prawns, thawed if frozen
1 cut-up fresh tomato for garnishing

serves 4 generously (F)

1. Put butter or margarine into a fairly
shallow 10 in/25 cm round glass or pottery
dish and melt 1–1½ mins at defrost setting.
Leave uncovered.
2. Stir in bacon, garlic and onions. Cover
with a plate and cook for 5 mins at full
power.
3. Stir in pimientos, canned tomatoes
(taking care not to break them up too
much), rice, paprika, turmeric and peas.
4. Stand chicken joints on top then brush
lightly with soy sauce.
5. Cover dish with cling film, then puncture
twice with the tip of a knife. Alternatively,
cover with matching lid. Cook 35 mins at
full power, turning dish 4 times unless oven
has a turntable.
6. Remove from oven, uncover, stud with
prawns and tomato, then serve.

ITALIAN-STYLE RISOTTO

Classic, as only an Italian dish can be, this Risotto contains the marrow from a beef bone, its fair share of wine and one of the country's most renowned cheeses – Parmesan – for sprinkling over the top.

---

2 oz/50 g butter

---

4 oz/125 g onions, peeled and chopped

---

1 oz/25 g beef bone marrow, sliced or diced

---

8 oz/225 g easy-cook, Italian round grain rice

¾ pt/425 ml boiling chicken stock

½ pt/275 ml dry white wine

---

4 saffron strands soaked in an egg cup of water

¼ level teaspoon salt

---

grated Parmesan cheese (about 2 oz/50 g)

---

serves 4 to 6 (F)

1. Put half the butter into a 3 pt/1.75 litre glass or pottery dish and melt for 1–1½ mins at defrost setting. Leave uncovered.
2. Stir in onions and bone marrow. Cook, uncovered, 5 mins at full power, stirring twice.
3. Mix in rice, boiling stock and the wine. Cover with a plate or matching lid and cook 14 mins at full power, stirring twice with a fork.
4. Uncover. Add rest of butter, saffron strands and liquid, salt and 1 oz/25 g Parmesan cheese.
5. Cook, uncovered, until rice grains have absorbed all the mixture; depending on the rice, this could take from 4–8 mins. Fork-stir at the end of every 2 mins, working gently to prevent breaking up the rice.
6. Spoon out on to plates and sprinkle each portion with rest of Parmesan cheese.

MACARONI CHICKEN CURRY

A useful and imaginative way of using up cold chicken, though any other kind of cooked meat may be used.

---

8 oz/225 g elbow macaroni

1½ pt/850 ml boiling water

---

1 rounded teaspoon salt

---

2 teaspoons salad oil

1½ oz/40 g butter or margarine

---

6 oz/175 g onions, peeled and chopped

---

3 oz/75 g red or green pepper, de-seeded and cut into small dice

---

1 oz/25 g plain flour

---

2 rounded teaspoons curry powder (mild or hot, depending on taste)

---

2 level tablespoons tubed or canned tomato purée

---

8 oz/225 g cold cooked chicken, cut into small cubes

¾ pt/425 ml chicken stock

¼ level teaspoon garlic salt

---

1 level teaspoon salt

---

1 level teaspoon turmeric

---

3 rounded tablespoons apple purée

---

serves 6

1. Put macaroni into a 3 pt/1.75 litre glass or pottery dish. Add boiling water, salt and oil. Cook, uncovered, for 15 mins at full power. Stir 3 times. Remove from oven. Stir again.
2. Cover with a plate and leave to stand while preparing chicken mixture. Put butter or margarine into a 3 pt/1.75 litre glass or pottery dish. Melt, uncovered, 1½–2 mins at defrost setting.
3. Mix in onions and pepper. Cover with a plate. Cook 3 mins at full power.
4. Gradually blend in rest of ingredients. Again cover with a plate and cook until very hot and thickened; 8–9 mins at full power, stirring 3 times.
5. Drain macaroni and transfer to serving dish. Spoon chicken mixture over the top. Accompany with chutney. If liked, garnish with lemon slices and parsley.

*Family Pasta Pot, served with cooked
red cabbage*

PASTA NEAPOLITAN

8 oz/225 g macaroni, shells, bows or any other shape

1½ pt/850 ml boiling water

1 level teaspoon salt

2 teaspoons salad oil

butter or margarine

SAUCE
1½ lb/675 g blanched tomatoes, skinned and cut into eighths

1 garlic clove, peeled and crushed

2 level tablespoons tubed or canned tomato purée

3 level teaspoons caster or soft brown sugar

½ level teaspoon salt

1 level teaspoon dried basil

1 heaped tablespoon chopped parsley

1 level tablespoon cornflour

1 tablespoon cold water

serves 4

1. Put pasta into a large glass or pottery dish. Add boiling water, salt and oil. Cook, uncovered 6–8 mins at full power, stirring gently twice. Remove from oven, cover and leave to stand 5 mins. Drain and toss in a little butter or margarine. Keep warm.
2. Put tomatoes, garlic and purée into food processor or blender goblet and run machine until smooth.
3. Pour into a 3 pt/1.75 litre glass or pottery dish. Mix in sugar, salt, basil and parsley.
4. Blend cornflour smoothly with water. Add to tomato mixture and stir in well.
5. Cover with a plate and cook 6 mins at full power, stirring 4 times. Leave to stand 4 mins. Reheat pasta 1–2 mins at full power.
6. Divide pasta between 4 warm serving dishes and top with sauce as desired. Pass grated cheese separately for sprinkling over top.

PASTA HAM CASSEROLE

A good companion to salad or cooked vegetables such as beans, peas, sprouts or even a mixture.

8 oz/225 g pasta shells

1½ pt/850 ml boiling water

1 rounded teaspoon salt

2 teaspoons salad oil

1 can condensed cream of mushroom soup

4 oz/125 g lean ham, chopped

4 oz/125 g button mushrooms, sliced

1 level teaspoon prepared mustard

seasoning to taste

4 oz/125 g Cheddar cheese, finely grated

serves 4

1. Put pasta shells into a large glass or pottery dish. Add boiling water, salt and oil. Cook, uncovered, for 10 mins at full power. Stir 3 times with spoon, taking care not to break up shells.
2. Remove from oven, cover with a plate and leave to stand for 10 mins. Drain and return to dish.
3. Stir in soup, ham, mushrooms and mustard. Season to taste with salt and pepper. Sprinkle with cheese.
4. Leave uncovered and re-heat 5 mins at full power, turning dish 3 times unless oven has a turntable.

MACARONI PEPPERONI

An uncomplicated macaroni accompaniment, flavoured with peppers and coloured with tomato juice. With grated cheese on each serving, and sprinkled with chopped parsley this becomes a main meal of some substance.

½ pt/275 ml tomato juice

4 oz/125 g elbow macaroni

1 level teaspoon salt

2 tablespoons hot wine or water

2 oz/50 g frozen diced green and red peppers (used from frozen)

1½ oz/40 g butter or margarine

TOPPING
3 oz/75 g Cheddar cheese, finely grated

1 heaped tablespoon chopped parsley

serves 2

1. Pour tomato juice into a 2 pt/1.25 litre glass or pottery dish. Cover with a plate. Heat until boiling, allowing about 2–3 mins at full power.
2. Take out of oven and stir in macaroni, salt, wine or water, the frozen vegetables and butter or margarine. Mix well. Cover with cling film, then puncture twice with the tip of a knife. Alternatively, cover with matching lid.
3. Cook 10 mins at full power, turning dish 4 times unless oven has a turntable. Leave to stand 5 mins before serving, topped with grated cheese and parsley.

SPAGHETTI WITH SWEET-SOUR PORK

8 oz/225 g spaghetti, snapped into thirds

1½ pt/850 ml boiling water

1 rounded teaspoon salt

2 teaspoons salad oil

1 oz/50 g butter or margarine

8 oz/225 g onion, peeled and chopped

12 oz/350 g pork fillet, cut into thin strips

¼ teaspoon dried minced garlic

1 rounded tablespoon tubed or canned tomato purée

1 level tablespoon cornflour

1 can (12 oz/340 g) pineapple chunks

3 oz/75 g red pepper, de-seeded and chopped

3 oz/75 g green pepper, de-seeded and chopped

¼ level teaspoon ginger

1 tablespoon soy sauce

salt and pepper to taste

serves 4

1. Put spaghetti into a 4 pt/2.25 litre glass or pottery dish. Add boiling water, salt and oil. Cook, uncovered, for 10 mins at full power. Stir at last 3 times. Remove from oven.
2. Cover with a plate and leave to stand while preparing sweet-sour mixture. Put butter or margarine into 3 pt/1.75 litre glass or pottery dish and melt 1–1½ mins at defrost setting. Add onions. Cover dish with plate and cook 2 mins at full power.
3. Gently stir in all remaining ingredients. Cover with a plate or matching lid. Cook 15 mins, stirring 3 times.
4. Reheat spaghetti for 2 mins. Drain. Spoon into a serving dish and top with sweet-sour pork mixture. Serve straight away.

LASAGNE VERDI

A classic Italian dish which is much improved in flavour if the Bolognese Sauce is cooked the day before

BOLOGNESE SAUCE

1 lb/450 g raw minced beef

1 garlic clove, peeled and crushed

4 oz/125 g onions, peeled and grated

4 oz/125 g green pepper, de-seeded and finely chopped

1 level teaspoon Italian seasoning or mixed herbs

1 can (14 oz/400 g) tomatoes, mashed down in their own liquid

2 rounded tablespoons tomato purée

1 brown gravy cube

5 tablespoons red wine or water

3 level teaspoons brown sugar

1 level teaspoon salt

CHEESE SAUCE

½ pt/275 ml milk, taken from the refrigerator

1 oz/25 g butter or margarine

1 oz/25 g plain flour

2–3 oz/50–75 g grated cheese

1 level teaspoon prepared mustard

seasoning to taste

6 oz/175 g green lasagne

1½ pt/850 ml boiling water

1 level teaspoon salt

2 teaspoons salad oil

1 oz/25 g grated Cheddar or Parmesan cheese

1 oz/25 g melted butter or margarine

paprika

serves 4–6 (F)

1. To make Bolognese Sauce, put beef and garlic into a 3 pt/1.75 litre glass or pottery dish. Thoroughly mix in onions and pepper. Leave uncovered and cook 5 mins at full power.
2. Stir in Italian seasoning or mixed herbs, the mashed tomatoes and liquid, tomato purée, crumbled gravy cube, wine or water and the sugar.
3. Cover with cling film, then puncture twice with the tip of a knife. Cook 15 mins at full power, turning dish twice unless oven has a turntable. Uncover, season with salt and stir round. Re-cover as above. Refrigerate when cold.
4. To make Cheese Sauce, pour milk into a glass or pottery jug. Leave uncovered and heat 1½ mins at full power until fairly hot. Remove from oven.
5. Put butter or margarine into a bowl. Leave uncovered and melt 1–1½ mins at defrost setting.
6. Stir in flour to form a roux and cook ½ min at full power. Remove from oven and gradually blend in the warm milk.
7. Return to oven and cook, uncovered, until sauce comes to the boil and thickens. Stir in cheese and mustard. Allow about 3 to 4 mins at full power and beat at the end of every min to ensure sauce stays smooth. Season to taste and stir well.
8. Cook 3–4 leaves of lasagne at a time so that it can move about in the liquid. Put leaves into a large glass or pottery dish with boiling water, salt and oil.
Leave uncovered and cook 12–15 mins at full power. Stir gently 4 times. Leave to stand 6–8 mins.
9. Top up water level if necessary for next batch of lasagne. Lift out onto a clean tea towel and leave to drain. When all the lasagne has been cooked, assemble the layers as directed below.
10. Grease an 8 in/20 cm square glass or pottery dish and fill with alternate layers of cooked lasagne, Bolognese Sauce and Cheese Sauce. Begin with lasagne and end with Cheese Sauce.
11. Top with cheese, melted butter or margarine and paprika. Reheat, uncovered, 10–15 mins at full power, time depending on whether the sauces are hot, warm or cold.

Fresh Ravioli in Fast Tomato Sauce

FRESH RAVIOLI IN FAST TOMATO SAUCE

Now that fresh pasta is available from some of the leading supermarket chains, why not make this easy-care version

9 oz/about 250 g fresh, meat-filled ravioli
1 pt/575 ml boiling water
1 can (8 oz/225 g) tomatoes
2 level tablespoons tomato purée
1 garlic clove, peeled and crushed
½ level teaspoon salt
½ level teaspoon granulated sugar
2 slightly rounded tablespoons chopped parsley

serves 4

1. Put ravioli and water into a 3 pt/1.75 litre dish. Leave uncovered.
2. Cook for 10 mins at full power, stirring twice with a wooden spoon. Stand for 5 mins inside or outside the oven, whichever is the most convenient. Drain
3. Tip tomatoes and their liquor into a basin and crush against the sides with a fork. Add rest of ingredients and mix well.
4. Toss gently into ravioli with a wooden spoon then cover with a dinner plate.
5. Cook for 4 mins at full power, turning dish twice unless oven has a turntable. Stir in cooked ravioli. Serve straight away while still very hot.

SPAGHETTI CARBONARA

Serve with a green salad tossed in a mild dressing and garnsh with black olives, capers and rolls of anchovy fillets.

8 oz/225 g spaghetti, snapped into thirds
1½ pt/850 ml boiling water
1 rounded teaspoon salt
2 teaspoon salad oil
7 oz/200 g lean bacon, chopped
2 tablespoons milk + 2 eggs (size 2) beaten together
4 oz/125 g Cheddar or Gruyère cheese, finely grated
4 tablespoons double cream
salt and pepper to taste
paprika

serves 6

1. Put spaghetti into a 3 pt/1.75 litre glass or pottery dish. Add boiling water, salt and oil. Cook, uncovered, for 15 mins at full power. Stir at least 3 times. Remove from oven.
2. Cover with a plate and leave to stand a further 5 mins when spaghetti should be more swollen and a little bit softer. Drain and return to dish. Re-cover with a plate to keep hot.
3. Put chopped bacon into a separate small dish. Cover with a plate and cook 4 mins at full power, stirring once.
4. Add to spaghetti with beaten milk and eggs, cheese, cream and seasoning to taste. Toss with 2 spoons. Cover with plate again then reheat 5 mins at full power to give egg and milk mixture a chance to scramble.
5. Uncover. Toss gently to mix and sprinkle with paprika. Serve straight away, while still very hot.

LENTIL DHAL

Distinctly oriental with origins in India, this Lentil Dhal is an elegantly-flavoured and nutritious dish which makes a fine meal with freshly cooked long grain rice and side dishes of yogurt, chutney and sliced onions.

8 oz/225 g orange lentils
2 oz/50 g butter or margarine, or 3 tablespoons salad oil
12 oz/350 g onions, peeled and chopped
1 garlic clove, peeled and crushed
1 rounded teaspoon turmeric
1 rounded teaspoon paprika
½ level teaspoon ground ginger
1 rounded tablespoon garam masala
⅛ level teaspoon cayenne pepper
4 cardamon pods, broken open to release seeds
1 rounded tablespoon tubed or canned tomato purée
1¼ pt/725 ml boiling water
1½ level teaspoons salt
fresh coriander leaves, chopped

serves 6 generously (F)

1. Rinse lentils under cold, running water. Leave on one side temporarily.
2. Put butter, margarine or oil into a 3 pt/1.75 litre dish and heat, uncovered, for 1 min at full power. Mix in onions and garlic. Cover with a plate. Cook 3 mins at full power.
3. Stir in rest of ingredients. Cover with cling film, puncturing twice with the tip of a knife. Cook 15 mins at full power, turning dish 3 or 4 times unless oven has a turntable.
4. Fluff up with a fork before serving and, if too thick for personal taste, add a little extra boiling water until the right consistency is achieved. Garnish by sprinkling with chopped coriander.

SULTAN'S SALAD

8 oz/225 g bulgar
1 pt/575 ml boiling water
1–1½ level teaspoons salt
6 oz/175 g cold, cooked lamb, chopped
1 peeled and crushed garlic clove
2 oz/50 g grated carrots
1 level tablespoon chopped fresh mint
4 rounded tablespoons chopped parsley
strained juice of 1 medium lemon
3–4 tablespoons corn or sunflower oil
pepper
olives, black and green, for garnish

serves 4

1. Put bulgar into an 8 in/20 cm round and fairly deep glass or pottery dish. Leave uncovered and toast, with no water, for 3 mins at full power, stirring at the end of every min.
2. Mix in boiling water. Cook, uncovered, for 5 mins at full power, stirring 3 times. Season to taste with salt then fluff up with a fork. Draining should be unnecessary as the bulgar will absorb the water in the cooking time recommended. Leave to cool until lukewarm.
3. Stir in rest of ingredients, adjust seasoning, with extra salt if required, and pepper. Spoon into a dish and stud with olives. Serve with Pitta bread.

KIBBLED WHEAT SALAD

8 oz/225 g kibbled wheat
1½ pt/850 ml hot water
1½ level teaspoons salt
1 tablespoon salad oil
juice of a small lemon
3 oz/75 g onion, peeled and finely grated
2 heaped tablespoons finely chopped parsley
2 oz/50 g toasted cashew nuts (microwave 3–4 mins at full power)
omelet strips for garnish

serves 4

1. Rinse kibbled wheat and put into a 4 pt/2.25 litre glass or pottery dish. Add hot water and salt.
2. Cover with cling film. Slit three times with a knife. Cook 10 mins at full power, turning dish 4 times unless oven has a turntable. Uncover.
3. Return to oven and cook at full power a further 15 mins, stirring 3 times.
4. Remove from oven, cover with a plate and leave until completely cold. Drain if necessary but wheat should have absorbed all the moisture.
5. Fork in rest of ingredients, transfer to a dish or bowl and serve garnished with omelet strips when cold.

PIZZAS NEAPOLITAN

2 tablespoons salad or olive oil
4 oz/125 g onions, peeled and chopped
1 garlic clove, peeled and crushed
5 oz/150 g tomato purée
white or brown risen bread dough
12 oz/350 g Mozzarella cheese, grated
2 oz/50 g anchovies in oil, drained and separated
4 oz/125 g small black olives

makes 4

1. Put oil, onions and garlic into a 1 pt/575 ml dish, leave uncovered and cook 5 mins at full power, stirring once.
2. Mix in tomato purée and leave on one side temporarily.
3. Knead dough lightly and divide into 4 equal pieces. Roll out into rounds, large enough to cover 4 greased and floured 8 in/20 cm dinner plates.
4. Ease dough out towards the edges then warm, one plate at a time, for ½ min at defrost setting. Rest 4 mins. Repeat 3 or 4 times or until dough doubles in size. Leave uncovered throughout.
5. Spread each with tomato mixture then top with grated cheese. Garnish attractively with anchovies and olives then cook individually, allowing 5 mins at full power and turning plate twice unless oven has a turntable. Serve piping hot.

RATATOUILLE

Serve with meat, egg and poultry dishes or, for vegetarian tastes, spoon over rice, pasta or bulgar. The flavour is improved if Ratatouille is cooked one day for the next and reheated, covered, for about 7 mins at full power. It may also be reheated on individual plates.

4 tablespoons salad oil
6 oz/175 g onions, peeled and chopped
1 garlic clove, peeled and crushed
8 oz/225 g courgettes, topped and tailed then washed and thinly sliced
12 oz/350 g aubergines, stem ends removed then washed and cubed wthout peeling
4 oz/125 g washed red or green pepper, de-seeded and chopped
½ can (7 oz/200 g) tomatoes
1 rounded tablespoon tomato purée
3 rounded teaspoons brown sugar
2 level teaspoons salt
2 heaped tablespoons chopped parsley

serves 6 to 8 (F)

1. Pour oil into a 4 pt/2.25 litre glass or pottery dish. Heat 1 min at full power. Leave uncovered.
2. Add onions and garlic. Mix in well then cook, uncovered, for 4 mins at full power.
3. Stir in courgettes, aubergines, red or green pepper, tomatoes, purée, sugar, half the salt and half the parsley. Cover with cling film, then puncture twice with the tip of a knife.
4. Cook for 20 mins at full power, turning dish 4 times unless oven has a turntable. Uncover and stir. Add rest of salt and parsley.
5. Leave uncovered and continue to cook 8–10 mins at full power or until most of the liquid has evaporated. Stir at least 4 times. Cool and cover.

DANISH-STYLE RED CABBAGE

I've said Danish, but cooked red cabbage is eaten throughout Scandinavia and Northern Europe. It is a winter speciality, a treat with pork or goose or even sausages, and bliss to cook in the microwave where it remains slightly crisp and bright-coloured – cooked conventionally, it dulls down and looks a bit like mahogany. One warning. The cabbage tends to stain the hands when shredding so use a food processor if you have one, or the shredding attachment of a mixer. The flavour will be more mature if cooked a day in advance.

Illustrated on page 68

2 lb/900 g red cabbage
¾ pt/425 ml boiling water
1½ level teaspoons salt
8 oz/225 g onions, peeled and finely chopped
8 oz/225 g peeled cooking apples, cored and chopped
2 level tablespoons light brown soft sugar
¼ level teaspoon caraway seeds
2 level tablespoons cornflour
3 tablespoons malt vinegar
1 extra tablespoon cold water

serves 6 to 8 (F)

1. Wash cabbage, taking off any outer damaged and/or bruised leaves. Cut cabbage into pieces, minus stalks, and shred as finely as possible.
2. Put into a 4 pt/2.25 litre glass or pottery dish with ½ pt/275 ml boiling water and 1 teaspoon salt. Mix thoroughly. Cover with a plate and cook 10 mins at full power.
3. Stir round then add rest of water, salt, onions, apples, sugar and caraway seeds. Mix thoroughly. Cover with cling film then puncture twice with the tip of a knife.
4. Cook 20 mins at full power, turning dish 4 times unless oven has a turntable. Remove from oven. Blend cornflour smoothly with vinegar and tablespoon of water.
5. Add to cabbage and stir well to mix. Leave uncovered and cook 10 mins at full power. Stir 4 times. Remove from oven and cover. Leave until cold then refrigerate overnight as this helps to mature the flavour. Reheat, covered, 5–6 mins before serving.

*Preparation of Danish-style Red
Cabbage*
Recipe on page 67

HERB GARDEN MOSAIC

*A lovely frozen vegetable mix for those occasions when you
are short of time and grateful for the bounty in the freezer*

Illustrated on page 69

---

8 oz/225 g frozen broad beans

---

8 oz/225 g frozen sliced courgettes

---

8 oz/225 g frozen sweetcorn

---

3 oz/75 g frozen mixed diced red and green
  peppers

---

4 oz/125 g frozen sliced onions

---

4 leaves of basil, chopped

---

2 leaves of mint, chopped

---

2 in/5 cm sprig of rosemary, 'needles' taken off
  stalks

---

2 in/5 cm sprig of savory, leaves taken off stalks

---

3 in/7.5 cm sprig of thyme, left as a sprig

1–2 oz/25–50 g butter or margarine

1½–2 level teaspoons salt

---

serves 6 to 8

1. Put all vegetables, used from frozen, into
a 3–3½ pt/2 litre glass or pottery dish,
stirring well to mix.
2. Cover with cling film, then puncture
twice with the tip of a knife. Alternatively,
cover with matching lid.
3. Cook 16 mins at full power, turning dish
twice unless oven has a turntable
4. Leave to stand 5 mins inside or outside
the oven, whichever is the most convenient.
Uncover. Drain off liquid then stir in the
fresh herbs and butter or margarine. Season
to taste with salt and serve hot.

Herb Garden Mosaic

JUNIPER COURGETTES

The inclusion of juniper berries adds a gin-like and unexpected note of subtlety to the courgettes, a most pleasing accompaniment to poultry and fish dishes.

1 oz/25 g butter or margarine

1 lb/450 g topped and tailed courgettes, washed and thinly sliced

6 juniper berries, lightly crushed with the back of a spoon

½ level teaspoon salt

1 heaped tablespoon finely chopped parsley

serves 4 to 5

1. Put butter or margarine in an 8 in/20 cm round glass or pottery dish and melt, uncovered, 1–1½ mins at defrost setting.
2. Stir in courgettes, juniper berries and salt and spread evenly into a layer that covers base of dish.
3. Cover with cling film then puncture twice with the tip of a knife. Cook 10 mins at full power, turning dish 4 times unless oven has a turntable.
4. Stand 2 mins before uncovering and sprinkling with parsley.

BUTTERED CHINESE LEAVES WITH PERNOD

Greatly enhanced by the addition of Pernod which adds a delicate and subtle note of aniseed.

1½ lb/675 g Chinese leaves, well-washed and shredded

2 oz/50 g butter or margarine, melted in microwave for 1½–2 mins

3 teaspoons Pernod

½ level teaspoon salt

serves 4

1. Mix all ingredients well together in a 3 pt/1.75 litre glass or pottery dish.
2. Cover with cling film, then puncture twice with the tip of a knife. Alternatively, cover with matching lid.
3. Cook 12 mins at full power, turning dish 4 times unless oven has a turntable. Leave to stand 5 mins then serve.

ORANGE BEETS

Hot beetroots in orange juice may sound unusual, but they make a lively accompaniment to pork, ham, duck and goose.

1 lb/450 g cooked beetroots, peeled and sliced

5 tablespoons fresh orange juice (reconstituted frozen is ideal)

1 tablespoon malt vinegar

½ level teaspoon salt

1 garlic clove, peeled and crushed

serves 4 to 6

1. Put beetroot slices into a fairly shallow, 7 in/17.5 cm round glass or pottery dish.
2. Beat together rest of ingredients. Pour over beetroot. Cover with cling film, then puncture twice with the tip of a knife.
3. Cook 6 mins at full power, turning dish twice unless oven has a turntable. Stand 1 min then serve hot.

BUTTERED LIME CARROTS

An all-occasion carrot dish, unusually brightened with lime cordial. Try it with veal, turkey, game dishes or offal.

2 oz/50 g butter or margarine

1 lb/450 g carrots, peeled and grated

4 oz/125 g onions, peeled and grated

1 tablespoon lime cordial

1 level teaspoon salt

serves 4 to 6 (F)

1. Put butter or margarine into an 8 in/ 20 cm round glass or pottery dish. Melt for 1½–2 mins at defrost setting. Leave uncovered.
2. Stir in carrots, onions, lime cordial and salt. Mix well and cover with cling film. Puncture twice with the tip of a knife.
3. Cook 15 mins at full power, turning dish 3 times unless oven has a turntable. Leave to stand 2 or 3 mins before serving.

SCALLOPED CELERIAC

Makes a grand accompaniment to meat, poultry, egg and fish dishes and is worth a try in the winter months when it is most readily available.

2 lb/900 g celeriac
½ pt/275 ml hot water
1 tablespoon lemon juice (added to prevent browning)
2 level teaspoons salt
2 oz/50 g lean bacon, chopped and microwaved for 1½ mins at full power
½ pt/275 ml single cream
1 oz/25 g potato crisps, crushed

serves 6

1. Peel celeriac thickly, wash well and cut each head into eighths. Put into 4 pt/2.25 litre dish with hot water, lemon juice and half the salt.
2. Cover with cling film then puncture twice with the tip of a knife. Cook 20 mins at full power, turning dish twice unless oven has a turntable. Drain then cut celeriac into cubes. Return to dish in which it was cooked. Gently mix in rest of salt, bacon and cream.
4. Sprinkle with potato crisps and cook, uncovered, 4 mins at full power, turning dish 3 times unless oven has a turntable.

CAULIFLOWER CAMELIA

Serve as a vegetable with beef, lamb, chicken, turkey, gammon or microwaved fish.

1½ lb/675 g head of cauliflower, weighed after leaves and most of the woody centre stalk have been cut off
4 tablespoons hot water
1 carton (5 oz/142 ml) soured cream
1 egg (size 2)
1 round teaspoon cornflour
2 teaspoons cold water
5 oz/150 g Cheshire cheese, grated
salt and pepper to taste
paprika

serves 4

1. Stand cauliflower upright in a deepish glass or pottery dish. Add hot water and cover with cling film. Puncture twice with the tip of a knife. Alternatively, cover with a matching lid.
2. Cook for 10 mins at full power, turning dish 4 times unless oven has a turntable.
3. Uncover and drain off water. Beat soured cream and egg well together then stir in cornflour, first smoothly mixed with cold water.
4. Stir in cheese then season to taste with salt and pepper. Spoon over cauliflower and sprinkle with paprika. Cover as before.
5. Cook a further 3 mins at full power, turning dish at the end of every min unless oven has a turntable. Stand 2 mins. Serve as suggested.

FENNEL WITH TARRAGON

A sophisticated vegetable with a mild aniseed flavour, fennel is companionable with fish or chicken

2 lb/900 g fennel
2 oz/50 g butter or margarine
½ level teaspoon salt
1 rounded teaspoon Bordeaux mustard
2 tablespoons medium sherry
½ level teaspoon tarragon

serves 4

1. Wash and dry fennel. Cut off any bruised or damaged pieces but leave on 'fingers' and 'fronds'.
2. Melt butter or margarine, uncovered in cup, for 1½–2 mins at defrost setting. Gently beat in salt, mustard, sherry and tarragon.
3. Cut each head of fennel into quarters, working from top to bottom and retaining 'fingers' and 'fronds'.
4. Arrange in a 10 in/25 cm round and fairly shallow glass or pottery dish. Coat with the butter or margarine mixture.
5. Cover with cling film, then puncture twice with the tip of a knife.
6. Cook for 20 mins at full power, turning dish twice unless oven has a turntable. Leave to stand for 7 mins inside or outside the oven, whichever is the most convenient.

Asparagus Hollandaise

ASPARAGUS HOLLANDAISE

---

1 lb/450 g asparagus spears

2 tablespoons water

½–1 level teaspoon salt

HOLLANDAISE SAUCE
4 oz/125 g slightly salted butter

1 tablespoon fresh lemon juice

2 egg yolks (size 3)

salt and pepper to taste

pinch of caster sugar

serves 4

1. Wash asparagus spears, leave whole and put into glass or pottery dish. Add water and salt. Cover with cling film, slit twice with the tip of a knife.
2. Cook 10 mins at full power (12 mins if spears are thick) Turn dish twice unless oven has a turntable. Drain then serve with Hollandaise Sauce (below).
3. To make sauce, put butter into a smallish jug or dish and leave uncovered. Melt until hot and bubbly for 1–1½ mins at full power.
4. Add lemon juice and egg yolks. Whisk well. Return to oven and cook 30 secs at full power.
5. Remove from oven and stir briskly. The sauce is ready if it is thick as cold custard and clings to whisk, fork or spoon – whichever implement you have used. If not, cook a further 15 secs.
6. Season with salt and pepper to taste, then add sugar to counteract sharpness coming from the lemon.

Compote of Arabian Nights
Recipe on page 84

BROCCOLI CHEESE SUPREME

Very attractively coloured, a base of deep green broccoli is covered with a rich cream sauce, tastefully flavoured with mustard then sprinkled with paprika and nutmeg. The stalks remain firm but do eat them as they are high in natural fibre.

1 lb/450 g broccoli
4 tablespoons water
1 level teaspoon salt
1 carton (5 oz/142 ml) soured cream
4 oz/125 g Cheddar cheese, grated
1 egg (size 3)
1 level teaspoon prepared mustard
½ level teaspoon paprika
¼ level teaspoon nutmeg

serves 4 to 6

1. Wash broccoli, separate into branches and arrange at each end of a 10½ × 8 × 3 in/ 27 × 20 × 7.5 cm dish with the flowery tops facing towards centre.
2. Add water and sprinkle with salt.
3. Cover with matching lid or cling film, puncturing the latter twice with the tip of a knife.
4. Cook 12 mins at full power, remove from oven and carefully drain.
5. Beat together remaining ingredients and spoon over broccoli. Cover as before. Cook a further 3 mins at full power. Uncover and serve.

SPICED AUBERGINE PURÉE

1 lb/450 g aubergines
4 tablespoons water
2 teaspoons lemon juice
½ oz/15 g melted butter or margarine
1 rounded tablespoon finely chopped fresh coriander
1–2 level teaspoons salt
⅛ teaspoon mixed spice
¼ level teaspoon paprika

serves 4

1. Cut tops (stem ends) off unpeeled aubergines and slice. Put into dish with water and ½–1 level teaspoon salt. Cover with plate or matching lid and cook for 6 mins at full power. Stir halfway through cooking.
2. Drain and work to a purée in blender goblet or food processor with the lemon juice.
3. Scrape into a dish and add butter or margarine, coriander, ½–1 level teaspoon salt, mixed spice and paprika.
4. Put into a serving dish, cover with a plate and reheat 2½–3 mins at full power. Stand 1–2 mins before eating.
The plain purée may be made ahead of time and left, uncovered, in the refrigerator before using. Either bring to kitchen temperature before mixing with the rest of the ingredients, or reheat for an extra ½–1 min at full power.

BUTTERED CUCUMBER

Cooked cucumber with its delicate crunch and pale green colour, is a tantalizing and unusual accompaniment for fish and chicken. A dinner party winner!

1 medium cucumber (about 1 lb/450 g), peeled
1 oz/25 g butter or margarine, at kitchen temperature
½ level teaspoon salt
1 rounded tablespoon finely chopped parsley

serves 4

1. Very thinly slice cucumber and wring dry in a tea towel.
2. Put butter into a fairly shallow glass or pottery dish measuring about 8 × 8 in/ 20 × 20 cm. Or use any other shaped dish of about 2 pt/1.25 litre capacity. Melt, uncovered, for 1–1½ mins at defrost setting.
3. Stir in cucumber and salt. Cover with an inverted plate, matching lid or cling film. If using film, puncture twice with tip of knife.
4. Cook 6 mins at full power, turning dish 4 times unless oven has a turntable. Uncover and stir in parsley. Serve straight away.

PERNOD ARTICHOKES

4 large globe artichokes

salted water for soaking

2 tablespoons Pernod

6 tablespoons water

1 garlic clove, peeled

1 rounded teaspoon salt

serves 4

1. To cook artichokes, cut away stalks, leaving bases flat. With a sharp and non-serrated knife, cut tops off upper leaves as though you were slicing a loaf of bread. You will find the easiest way to do this is to place each artichoke on its side.
2. Soak for 20 mins in cold, salted water. Lift out and shake to remove surplus liquid.
3. Pour Pernod and water into a large dish, about 10 inches square by 2 inches in depth (25 by 5 cm). Crush in garlic then stir in salt. Add artichokes, placing them upright with leaves facing.
4. Cover with cling film, then puncture twice with the tip of a knife. Alternatively, cover with matching lid.
5. Cook 25 mins at full power, turning dish 4 times unless oven has a turntable. Leave to stand 10 mins. Uncover and leave until cold.
6. To prepare artichokes for guests, gently case leaves apart until you come to the centre. Remove core of inedible leaves and the spiky choke, then fill with French dressing.

CREAMED SWEET POTATOES

1 lb/450 g sweet potatoes or yams

4 tablespoons boiling water

½–1 oz/15–25 g butter or margarine

3–4 tablespoons warm milk.

seasoning

serves 4

1. Peel and dice potatoes and put into a 1¾ pt/1 litre dish. Add water. Cover with cling film, then puncture twice with the tip of a knife. Alternatively, cover with matching lid.
2. Cook 10 mins at full power, turning dish 4 times unless oven has a turntable. Leave to stand 2–3 mins, drain and mash finely.
3. Cream with butter or margarine and milk, season to taste and put into a serving dish. Reheat 1–1½ mins at full power. Covering is unnecessary.

CHÂTEAU POTATOES

If you are able to slice the potatoes in a food processor, so much the better. If not, use a grater or cut into hair-thin wafers with a very sharp knife.

2 lb/900 g potatoes, peeled and cut into wafer thin slices

1 garlic clove, peeled and crushed, mixed with 3 oz/75 g butter or margarine, melted

6 oz/175 g grated cheese – Gruyère or Emmental are ideal but for greater economy, use Cheddar or Edam

1 level teaspoon salt

pepper to taste

½ pt/275 ml medium cider

paprika

serves 6 (F)

1. Grease a 10 in/25 cm round glass or pottery dish, of about 2 ins/5 cm in depth, with butter or margarine.
2. Fill with alternate layers of potatoes, two-thirds of the garlic and butter or margarine mixture, and the same amount of cheese. Begin and end with potatoes and sprinkle salt and pepper between layers.
3. Gently pour cider down side of dish. Trickle rest of butter over the top then sprinkle with remaining cheese. Add a light dusting of paprika.
4. Cover with cling film, then puncture twice with the tip of a knife. Alternatively, cover with a matching lid.
5. Cook for 20 mins at full power, turning dish 4 times unless oven has a turntable. Leave to stand 5 mins in the oven, uncover and serve.

BEAN SPROUTS IN CHINESE-STYLE SAUCE

Well worth a try as an accompaniment to omelets or Chinese dishes, be they homemade or take-away. The sprouts are also appetizing with chicken.

1 lb/450 g fresh bean sprouts

2 tablespoons soy sauce

1 teaspoon Worcestershire sauce

1 level teaspoon onion salt

serves 4

1. Toss all ingredients well together in a bowl. Transfer to an 8 in/20 cm round glass or pottery dish that is fairly deep.
2. Cover with cling film, then puncture twice with the tip of a knife.
3. Cook 5 mins at full power, turning dish twice unless oven has a turntable. Uncover, stir round and serve.

PAPRIKA MUSHROOMS

Makes a regal meal with baby boiled potatoes or small pasta

2 lb/900 g button mushrooms

2 oz/50 g butter or margarine

1 garlic clove, peeled and crushed

1 large carton (10 oz or 284 ml) soured cream

1 level tablespoon paprika

1 rounded tablespoon tubed or canned tomato
    purée

1 ½ level teaspoon salt

serves 6

1. Trim mushrooms then wash and dry.
2. Put butter or margarine into a 4 pt/2.25 litre glass or pottery dish and melt 1½–2 mins at defrost setting. Leave uncovered.
3. Add mushrooms and garlic. Cover with a plate and cook 10 mins at full power, stirring 3 times.
4. Mix in remaining ingredients, tossing over and over gently with a spoon. Cover as above. Cook 5 mins at full power, stirring once.
5. Remove from oven and uncover. Stir once more then serve with suggested accompaniments.

SOUR CABBAGE

Takes a while to cook conventionally – about 1½ to 2 hours – but the microwave does a magnificent job in about half that time at defrost setting. Like the red cabbage from Denmark, this one is also best cooked one day for the next and is not unlike mild sauerkraut. You will find the cabbage takes on a creamy gold colour and stays very slightly crisp.

2 lb/900 g white cabbage

6 tablespoons water

4 tablespoons malt vinegar

2 rounded tablespoons granulated sugar

2 level teaspoons caraway seeds

1 ½ level teaspoons salt

serves 8 to 10 (F)

1. Wash cabbage, taking off any outer damage and/or bruised leaves. Cut cabbage into pieces, minus stalk, and shred as finely as possible.
2. Put into a 4 pt/2.25 litre dish with all remaining ingredients. Stir well to mix. Cover with cling film, then puncture twice with the tip of a knife.
3. Cook ¾ hour at defrost setting, turning dish 4 times unless oven has a turntable. Cool and leave out at kitchen temperature overnight.
4. Before serving, reheat individual portions on side plates, covering with kitchen paper and allowing about 1 min each at full power.

Left to right

Muesli Toffee Triangles, Best Brownies,
Dutch-style Cinnamon Shortbread
Recipes on pages 86 and 87

CALYPSO PUDDING

One of those soft and comforting puddings, always welcome in the depth of winter with an overcoat of hot custard. It cooks in around 8 mins.

---

8 oz/225 g self-raising flour

---

4 oz/125 g butter or margarine (or mixture), at room temperature

---

4 oz/125 g caster sugar

---

2 eggs (size 2) well-beaten

---

5 rounded tablespoons crushed pineapple with syrup

---

1 tablespoon liquid coffee and chicory essence

---

serves 4 to 5

1. Well-grease a 3 pt/1.75 litre straight-sided round dish. A glass or pottery soufflé dish is ideal.
2. Sift flour into a bowl. Rub in fats finely. Toss in sugar.
3. Using a fork, stir to a soft consistency with the eggs, pineapple and coffee.
4. Spread smoothly into prepared dish. Leave uncovered and cook 6½ mins at full power, turning dish 3 times unless oven has a turntable.
5. Invert on to a plate and if centre looks tacky, return to oven and cook an extra 1–1¼ mins.
6. Spoon into bowls and coat with hot custard.

BLACKCURRANT STODGE PUDDING

Good with thick cream!

---

10 oz/275 g self-raising flour

---

5 oz/150 g butter or margarine, at kitchen temperature

---

4 oz/125 g soft brown sugar

---

2 eggs (size 3) beaten

---

1 can (about 14 oz/200 g) blackcurrant pie filling

---

3 tablespoons cold milk

---

serves 6

1. Well-grease a 3 pt/about 1.75 litre round soufflé-type glass or pottery dish.
2. Sift flour into a bowl. Rub in butter or margarine finely. Toss in sugar.
3. Mix to a soft consistency with eggs, pie filling and cold milk, stirring briskly with a fork.
4. Spoon in prepared dish. Leave uncovered and cook 9 mins at full power, turning dish 3 times unless oven has a turntable.
5. Stand 5 mins, turn out on to a warm dish and spoon into portions.

'MULLED' PINEAPPLE

---

8 oz/225 g caster sugar

¼ pt/150 ml cold water

---

1 whole pineapple (about 4 lb/2 kg)

---

6 cloves

---

2 in/5 cm piece of cinnamon stick

⅛ teaspoon nutmeg

---

4 tablespoons ruby port

---

1 tablespoon brandy

---

serves 8 to 10

1. Put sugar and water into a 4 pt/2.25 litre dish. Stir round and cover with a plate. Cook 8 mins at full power.
2. Meanwhile, peel pineapple and cut flesh into wedges. Removal of centre core is a matter of personal choice but is not necessary.
3. Add to dish with rest of ingredients. Stir well to mix. Cover with cling film, then puncture twice with the tip of a knife.
4. Cook 10 mins at full power, turning dish 3 or 4 times unless oven has a turntable.
5. Remove from microwave, leave until cold then refrigerate overnight. Before serving, bring back to room temperature and spoon into dishes.

TIP *The pineapple may be served hot but is not as flavoursome*

FRESH RASPBERRY CREAM CRESCENT

A dream of a sweet, this would be impossible to make in a conventional oven, so the microwave triumphs yet again! It consists of a walnut 'omelet' based on egg whites, folded round double cream and raspberries.

3 egg whites (size 2)

⅛ teaspoon lemon juice

6 oz/175 g caster sugar

3 oz/75 g walnuts, finely ground in blender or food processor

¼ pt/150 ml double cream

8 oz/225 g raspberries, crushed

icing sugar

serves 6

1. Line the base of an 8 in/20 cm round glass or pottery dish, no taller than 2–3 ins/5–7.5 cm, with non-stick parchment paper. For safety and to prevent sticking, lightly grease the inside of the dish first.
2. Whisk egg whites and lemon juice together until very stiff. Gradually beat in sugar and continue beating until meringue is thick and heavy in texture. Fold in walnuts with a metal spoon.
3. Spread smoothly into the prepared dish. Leave uncovered and cook 5 mins at full power, turning dish once. Remove from microwave, leave until lukewarm then invert on to a piece of foil or greaseproof paper sprinkled thickly with sifted icing sugar.
4. When completely cold, remove lining paper. Whip cream until thick and gently fold in raspberries. Pile over one half of the walnut 'omelet'. Fold over so that the filling shows, dust with extra icing sugar and transfer to a serving dish. Chill lightly in the refrigerator before serving.

LEMON CHEESECAKE

A party-sized cheesecake with a dairy fresh flavour and moist, creamy texture. It is best made one day and eaten the next, left in the refrigerator about 12 hours to firm up.

BASE:
3 oz/75 g butter, at kitchen temperature

6 oz/175 g digestive biscuits, crushed

2 oz/50 g caster sugar

FILLING:
2 packets each 7 oz/200 g cream cheese or 1 lb/450 g medium fat curd cheese (available from delicatessens and some supermarkets)

3 oz/75 g caster sugar

2 eggs (size 1 or 2) at kitchen temperature

1 teaspoon vanilla essence

1 level tablespoon cornflour

finely grated peel and juice of 1 lemon weighing 4 oz/125 g

¼ pt/150 ml double cream

1 carton 15 oz/142 ml soured cream

serves 10

1. Melt butter, uncovered, for 2–2½ mins at defrost setting. Stir in biscuit crumbs and sugar. Line an 8 × 2 in/20 × 5 cm round glass or pottery dish with cling film. Cover base and sides evenly (and the evenly bit is quite important otherwise parts of the cake will be more crusty on the outside than others) with biscuit mixture, bringing it right to the top of the dish. Leave uncovered and cook 2½ mins at full power.
2. For filling, beat cheese until soft and light then whisk in sugar, eggs, essence, cornflour, lemon peel, lemon juice and the unwhipped cream.
3. When smooth and evenly combined, pour into crumb crust case. Cook 10–12 mins at full power, turning 4 times unless oven has a turntable. The cake is ready when there is some movement to be seen in the middle and the top rises up slightly and just begins to crack.
4. Remove from oven and spread with soured cream which will set on top as the cake evens out and cools.

Lemon Cheesecake
Recipe on page 79

FRUIT AND NUT BUTTER CHEESECAKE

I think this is one of my best cheescakes to date, a rich and creamy affair studded boldly with almonds and raisins, and tastefully flavoured with fresh lime juice.

6 oz/175 g crunchy oat biscuits or digestives, crushed

3 oz/75 g butter, melted (covered, in microwave 2–2½ mins, defrost setting)

1 lb/450 g curd cheese (from delicatessens), at kitchen temperature

4 oz/125 g caster sugar

1 level tablespoon cornflour

3 eggs (size 3) beaten

½ teaspoon vanilla essence

1 tablespoon fresh lime juice (about ¼ lime)

1 oz/25 g flaked almonds, lightly browned (in microwave 2–3 mins full power)

2 oz/50 g raisins

serves 8 to 10

1. Well-butter an 8 × 2 in/20 × 5 cm round dish. Cover base with all the crushed biscuits.
2. In mixing bowl, beat together butter, cheese, sugar, cornflour and eggs.
3. Stir in essence and lime juice. Crumble in the almonds and add raisins. Mix well. Spoon into dish over crumbs.
4. Cook for 24 mins, uncovered, at defrost setting, turning dish 4 times unless oven has a turntable.
5. Remove from oven and cool. Refrigerate at least 6 hours before cutting.

HONEYED RASPBERRY MARSHMALLOW DREAM

1 lb/450 g raspberries, thawed if frozen

3 slightly rounded tablespoons clear honey

1 packet (about 4½ oz/240 g) pink and white marshmallows

serves 6

1. Put raspberries and honey into a 3 pt/1.75 litre dish. Cover with a plate and cook 5 mins at full power, turning twice.
2. Remove from oven and uncover. Arrange marshmallows close together on top, forming a wide border.
3. Leave uncovered and cook a further 3 mins at full power. If serving cold, cool off in the kitchen, cover and refrigerate about 8 hours. If serving hot, spoon out on to plates and eat straight away.

NECTARINE AND BLUEBERRY CRUMBLE

1 lb/450 g nectarines

8 oz/225 g blueberries, washed

4 tablespoons cold water

3 oz/75 g caster sugar

TOPPING
6 oz/175 g wholewheat flour

3 oz/75 g butter or margarine, at kitchen temperature

2 level teaspoons cinnamon

3 oz/75 g Demarara sugar

serves 6 (F)

1. Puncture skin of nectarines by nicking once or twice with a knife. Put into bowl and cover with boiling water. Leave 2 mins. Drain and cover with cold water. Drain again and remove skins.
2. Cut each nectarine in half then twist to separate. Remove stones and cut flesh into slices. Put into a buttered glass or pottery soufflé-type dish, about 3 pt/1.75 litre.
3. Mix in blueberries and water. Cover with cling film, then puncture twice with the tip of a knife. Alternatively, cover with a matching lid.
4. Cook 5 mins at full power, turning dish 3 times unless oven has a turntable. Uncover, add sugar and stir until melted.
5. For crumble, put flour into a bowl. Rub in butter or margarine finely. Toss in cinnamon and sugar. Sprinkle thickly over fruit mixture. Leave uncovered.
6. Cook 4 mins at full power, turning 4 times unless oven has a turntable. Remove from oven, stand 2 mins then spoon on to plates.

SHERRY TRIFLE

A trifle, but this one is much, much better than average and closer to the grand affairs of yesteryear which our elders would have us believe were infinitely superior to modern copies! And maybe it's true. In my version of edible Victoriana, real Egg Custard sauce is the base, apricots the fruit, sherry the flavour, cream and chocolate the decorations. it's rich and lavish, a pretty party piece to show off with and lovely as a festive sweet for Christmas or Easter – or both.

CUSTARD SAUCE

1 pt/575 ml milk (long life gives an enriched flavour), or use half milk and half single cream

3 level teaspoons cornflour (prevents curdling as it acts as stabilizer)

1 tablespoon cold water

4 eggs (size 2)

2 rounded tablespoons caster sugar

1 teaspoon vanilla essence

2 Swiss rolls, jam filled and thinly sliced

1 can (14½ oz/420 g) apricot halves, drained

2 tablespoons sweet sherry

¼ pt/150 ml double cream

1 rounded tablespoon caster sugar

about 2 oz/50 g plain chocolate (left as a bar and not broken up)

serves 6 to 8

1. To make the custard sauce: heat milk, uncovered in jug, for 2 mins at full power.
2. Meanwhile, tip cornflour into a 2 pt/ 1 litre bowl, add water and stir until smooth. Break in eggs individually then add sugar.
3. Whisk until smooth then gradually blend in the hot milk. Leave uncovered. Cook 5–5½ mins at full power, whisking at the end of every min. When ready, custard should cling to the wooden fork or spatula used for whisking or, in the case of a wooden spoon, coat the back of it in an even layer. Mix in vanilla.
4. Press 6 slices of Swiss roll against the sides of a round, glass serving bowl about 8 ins/20 cm in diameter and no taller than 3 ins/7½ cm.
5. Reserve 6 apricot halves for decoration. Coarsely chop remainder. Almost fill centre of bowl with broken-up Swiss roll slices and apricots. Soak with sherry and 4 tablespoons apricot syrup.
6. Pour just over half the hot custard into the bowl, making sure it coats the sides of the Swiss roll and also the cake and fruit in the middle. Spoon rest of custard over the top. Cover and cool.
7. Chill 3–4 hours in the refrigerator. Before serving, decorate top edge with reserved apricot halves. Whip cream until thick, sweeten with sugar then pipe or spoon whirls or mounds in between the fruit.
8. Decorate middle with chocolate curls, made by standing chocolate on one long edge and running a vegetable peeler towards you along the opposite edge. Hold bar securely.

SOUFFLÉ OMELET

Dreamy and soft, filled with jam and showered with icing sugar – a perfect sweet to end a light meal.

2 oz/50 g jam, flavour to taste

icing sugar

melted butter

3 eggs (size 1 or 2)

3 drops lemon juice

1 rounded tablespoon caster sugar

serves 2

1. Spoon jam into a small dish or cup. Cover with a saucer and heat for 1½ mins at defrost setting. Remove from oven (it retains heat well) and leave to stand while preparing omelet. Cover a large piece of greaseproof paper with a thickish layer of sifted icing sugar.
2. Brush a 10 in/25 cm round and fairly shallow dish all over with melted butter.
3. Separate eggs, putting yolks into one bowl and whites into another. Add lemon juice to whites and beat until stiff.
4. Add sugar to egg yolks and whip to a thick cream. Gently whisk into egg whites. When thoroughly combined, spoon into prepared dish.
5. Cook, uncovered, for 3½ mins at full power, turning once unless oven has a turntable.
6. Invert on to the sugared paper, make a cut down the centre and spread one half with the warmed jam.
7. Fold in half and cut into 2 portions. Eat straight away.

LEMON FLOSS

Not for haute cuisiners but certainly for Mum, Dad and the children who all look forward to something light and refreshing at the end of a filling meal. It's nourishing too.

CUSTARD SAUCE

½ pt/275 ml milk (long life gives an enriched flavour), or use half milk and half single cream

1½ level teaspoons cornflour (prevents curdling as it acts as stabilizer)

½ tablespoon cold water

2 eggs (size 2)

1 rounded tablespoon caster sugar

½ teaspoon vanilla essence

1 lemon flavour jelly (4¾oz–135 g)

hot water

2 eggs (size 2) separated

½ teaspoon lemon juice

hundreds and thousands for decoration

serves 4 generously

1. To make the custard sauce, heat milk, uncovered in jug, for 1 min at full power.
2. Meanwhile, tip cornflour into a glass or pottery bowl, add water and stir until smooth. Break in eggs individually then add sugar.
3. Whisk until smooth then gradually blend in the hot milk. Leave uncovered. Cook 3–3½ mins at full power, whisking at the end of every min. When ready, custard should cling to the wooden fork or spatula used for whisking or, in the case of a wooden spoon, coat the back of it in an even layer. Mix in vanilla.
4. Divide jelly up into cubes and put into a measuring jug. Cover with a saucer. Melt for 2–2½ mins at defrost setting.
5. Make up to ½ pt/275 ml with hot water then whisk into the Egg Custard sauce. Follow by beating in yolks.
6. Cover. Leave until cold then refrigerate until just beginning to thicken and set.
7. Whisk egg whites and lemon juice to a stiff snow. Beat one-third into jelly mixture then fold in remainder.
8. Divide equally between 4 dishes and set in the refrigerator. Sprinkle with hundreds and thousands before serving.

LOUISIANA SPICE PIE

shortcrust pastry made with 6 oz/175 g plain flour and 3 oz/75 g fat etc

1 egg yolk, beaten

FILLING

1 lb/450 g sweet potatoes or yams

4 tablespoons boiling water

3 oz/75 g caster sugar

1 rounded teaspoon mixed spice

3 eggs (size 2)

¼ pt/150 ml cold milk

1 oz/25 g melted butter

serves 8

1. Roll out pastry fairly thinly and use to line a 8 in/20 cm glass or pottery fluted flan dish. Prick well all over, especially where sides join base.
2. Cook, uncovered, for 6 mins at full power, turning dish 4 times unless oven has a turntable. If pastry has bulged in places, press down very gently with fingers protected by oven gloves.
3. Brush all over with yolk to seal up holes then cook, uncovered, a further min at full power. Remove from oven and leave to stand temporarily while preparing filling.
4. Peel and dice potatoes and put into a 1¾ pt/1 litre dish. Add 4 tablespoons boiling water. Cover with cling film, then puncture twice with the tip of a knife. Alternatively, cover with matching lid.
5. Cook 10 mins at full power, turning dish 4 times unless oven has a turntable. Leave to stand 2–3 mins, drain and mash finely or, for smoother texture, work to a purée in blender goblet or food processor.
5. Tip into bowl and leave until cold. Add remaining ingredients and beat well until smoothly mixed. Spoon into pastry case, leave uncovered.
6. Cook for 22–25 mins at defrost setting, when filling should be set, turning 4 times unless oven has a turntable. Leave until just warm then cut into portions and serve topped with lightly whipped cream or vanilla ice cream.

COMPOTE OF ARABIAN NIGHTS

A 7-minute wonder

Illustrated on page 73

1 lb/450 g fresh *dates, at their best during the winter months*

1 lb/450 g bananas, *just ripe but not bruised*

juice of ½ medium *lemon*

3 tablespoons apricot *brandy*

½ teaspoon rose *flavouring essence*

1 rounded tablespoon demerara *sugar*

serves 6

1. Skin dates, slit each in half and remove stones. Put into a 3 pt/1.75 litre serving dish.
2. Peel bananas and slice directly on top of dates. Sprinkle with lemon juice then add apricot brandy and rose essence.
3. Toss gently together and sprinkle with the sugar. Cover with cling film, then puncture twice with the tip of a knife.
4. Cook 7 mins at full power, turning dish 3 times unless oven has a turntable. Serve warm with sponge cake.

CRANBERRY PARFAIT

A luscious dessert. And so easy.

SAUCE
8 oz/225 g cranberries, *thawed if frozen*

¼ pt/150 ml *water*

6 oz/175 g caster *sugar*

1 level teaspoon finely grated lemon *peel*

½ pt/275 ml double *cream*

2 tablespoons *milk*

serves 6

1. To make sauce: put first 4 ingredients in a 2 pt/1.25 litre dish. Cover with a plate.
2. Cook 8½ mins at full power, stirring sauce twice and crushing fruit against sides of bowl as you do so.
3. Remove from oven, keep covered. Leave until completely cold.
4. Whip cream and milk until thick. Fold in the Cranberry Sauce then divide mixture between 6 dishes. Refrigerate at least 2 hours before serving.

ORANGE EGG CUSTARD

½ pt/275 ml evaporated milk *or single cream (for extra richness)*

3 eggs *(size 3)*

1 extra egg yolk *(size 3)*

4 oz/125 g caster *sugar*

1 teaspoon vanilla *essence*

2 level teaspoons finely grated orange *peel*

½ level teaspoon *nutmeg*

serves 3 to 4

1. Pour milk or cream into a jug. Leave uncovered and warm 1½–2 mins at full power.
2. Whisk in eggs, egg yolk, sugar and vanilla essence. Strain into a 1¾ pt/1 litre buttered glass or pottery dish and stir in orange peel. Stand in a second dish, capacity 3–3½ pt/2 litre.
3. Pour sufficient boiling water into the large dish until it reaches the level of custard in the smaller dish.
4. Sprinkle top of custard with nutmeg then cook for 6–8 mins at full power when custard should be only just set.
5. Take smaller dish of custard out of the larger dish and wipe the sides dry. Leave to stand until centre has set. Serve warm or cold.

FESTIVE APPLE SNOW

As a change from the abundant foods of Christmas, this lighter dessert should be well-received, flavoured as it is with apple purée and the ever popular vanilla.

1 packet (1.1 oz/31 g) vanilla blancmange powder
$\frac{3}{4}$ pt/425 ml cold milk
3 level tablespoons caster sugar
4 oz/125 g apple purée
2 egg whites (size 2)
2–3 drops lemon juice

serves 4

1. Tip blancmange powder into a 2 pt/1.75 litre bowl and mix smoothly with 4 tablespoons of the measured milk.
2. Heat rest of milk, uncovered, for 4 mins at full power. Blend with blancmange mixture then stir in the sugar.
3. Return to oven and cook, uncovered, at full power until mixture boils and thickens; about $2\frac{1}{2}$ mins. Beat at the end of every $\frac{1}{2}$ min to ensure smoothness.
4. Remove from oven and whisk in the apple purée. Cool to lukewarm. Beat egg whites to a stiff snow with lemon juice. Fold into blancmange mixture gently and smoothly with a large metal spoon.
5. Spread evenly into a bowl then cover and chill several hours.

ORCHARD FRUIT CRUSH

Quite splendid with a topping of whipped cream, dusted prudently with very finely grated lemon peel and cinnamon

1 tangerine flavour packet jelly ($4\frac{3}{4}$ oz/135 g)
4 tablespoons boiling water
8 oz/225 g blackberries, washed and crushed with a fork
apple juice (I use Copella, available from some supermarkets and health food shops)
4 rounded tablespoons whipped cream
1 rounded teaspoon grated lemon peel
$\frac{1}{2}$ level teaspoon cinnamon

serves 4

1. Divide jelly up into cubes and put into a measuring jug with water. Cover with saucer. Melt for $2–2\frac{1}{2}$ mins at defrost setting.
2. Stir in blackberries then make up to 1 pt/575 ml with apple juice. Leave until cold.
3. Refrigerate, covered, until just beginning to thicken and set. Spoon into 4 dishes and leave in refrigerator until firm.
4. Top with cream then sprinkle with the lemon peel and cinnamon.

CHOCOLATE PEAR ADVOCAAT MOUSSE

A heady confection for special occasions

2 level teaspoons gelatine
2 tablespoons cold water
1 bar $3\frac{1}{2}$ oz/100 g plain chocolate
2 eggs (size 3) separated
$\frac{1}{4}$ pt/150 ml advocaat
1 can (15 oz/425 g) pear halves in juice or syrup, drained
2 level tablespoons chopped walnuts

serves 6

1. Shower gelatine into a small glass bowl. Add water. Stir round and cover with a saucer. Heat $1\frac{1}{2}$–$1\frac{3}{4}$ mins at defrost setting.
2. Remove from oven and stir round to ensure gelatine has dissolved. Leave aside temporarily.
3. Break up chocolate and put into a bowl. Leave uncovered and heat for $3–3\frac{1}{2}$ mins at defrost setting, stirring once. Add gelatine, egg yolks and advocaat then beat in well.
4. Cover and refrigerate until just beginning to thicken and set. Beat egg whites to a stiff snow. With a large metal spoon, gently fold into chocolate mixture.
5. Divide drained pears between 6 sundae dishes then top with chocolate mousse. Sprinkle with nuts and refrigerate until set.

WINE GLASS FRUIT 'SOUFFLÉS'

A surprise package, this one, steaming little 'soufflés' being served straight from the microwave in elegant, stemmed wine glasses.

1 can (14 oz/400 g) redcurrant and raspberry fruit filling (or other fruit filling to taste)

3 eggs (size 3) separated

6 tablespoons whipping cream

serves 6

1. Spoon fruit filling into a bowl and beat in egg yolks.
2. Beat egg whites to a stiff snow. Using a large metal spoon, gently and lightly fold into the fruit mixture.
3. Spoon into 6 stemmed wine glasses so that they are half-filled with mixture.
4. Cook in pairs for 3 mins at defrost setting when mixture should rise to top of each glass.
5. Remove from microwave. Make a slit in the top of each 'soufflé' with a knife then top with cream which will flow down the side of the glass and then to the base. Serve straight away.

NOTE *'Souffles' fall slightly on removal from the microwave*

CHERRY PETITS FOURS

Ideal for serving with after-dinner coffee

1 bar (3½ oz/100 g) plain chocolate

2 oz/50 g digestive biscuits, finely crushed

6 glacé cherries, halved

makes about 12

1. Break up chocolate, put into a bowl and melt 3–3½ mins at defrost setting. Leave uncovered.
2. Stir in biscuits then transfer equal amounts to 12 paper sweet cases.
3. Top with halved cherries and leave in the cool until quite firm before serving.

DUTCH-STYLE CINNAMON SHORTBREAD

The addition of semolina to the ingredients, and a different method of making, results in a crisp shortbread with a slightly coarse-grained texture.

Illustrated on page 77

11 oz/325 g plain flour

3 rounded teaspoons cinnamon

1 oz/25 g semolina

8 oz/225 g butter, at kitchen temperature

4 oz/125 g caster sugar

double cream

1 oz/25 g flaked and toasted almonds (microwave 2–3 mins full power)

extra caster sugar

cuts into 12 wedges

1. Sift flour into a bowl with cinnamon then toss in semolina. Rub in butter finely. Add sugar.
2. Knead by hand to a dough and spread over a buttered round glass or pottery dish measuring 8 × 2 ins/20 × 5 cm. Use fingers to ease dough over base of dish then spread evenly with a knife to make sure there are no thin patches.
3. Prick well all over with a fork. Brush top with double cream and allow to sink in. Press almonds into top for decoration. Leave uncovered and cook 20 mins at defrost setting, turning dish 4 times.
4. Remove from oven and sprinkle with 2–3 level teaspoons extra caster sugar.
5. Cut into 12 wedges and leave in the dish until cold. Carefully lift out and store in an airtight container.

BEST BROWNIES

Moist and out-of-this-world are the only ways in which I can describe these American-style chocolate squares, my best yet.

Illustrated on page 77

---

3 oz/75 g self-raising flour

---

1 oz/25 g cocoa powder

---

4 oz/125 g butter or margarine, at kitchen temperature

---

8 oz/225 g dark brown soft sugar

---

1 teaspoon vanilla essence

---

2 eggs (size 3) at kitchen temperature

---

3 tablespoons milk

---

icing sugar for the top

---

makes 12 (F)

1. Line an oblong dish, with a base measurement of 12 × 6 ins/30 × 15 cm, smoothly with cling film.
2. Sift flour and cocoa powder on to a plate. Put butter or margarine and sugar into a bowl. Add essence and beat until creamy and soft.
3. Beat in eggs individually then, with a metal spoon, stir in flour mixture alternately with milk.
4. When evenly combined, spread smoothly into the prepared dish and cover with cling film. Puncture twice with the tip of a knife.
5. Cook for 6 mins at full power, turning dish once unless oven has a turntable. Remove from oven and remove cling film cover. Leave Brownies in the dish until lukewarm.
6. Lift out, with cling film lining, on to a wire rack. Allow to cool completely, cut into 12 squares and turn upside down. Sprinkle thickly with icing sugar before serving. Store leftovers in an airtight container.

MUESLI TOFFEE TRIANGLES

Illustrated on page 77

---

4 oz/125 g butter

---

2 oz/50 g golden syrup

---

1 oz/25 g black treacle

---

4 oz/125 g dark brown soft sugar

---

8 oz/225 g unsweetened *muesli mix*

---

1. Well-grease an 8 in/20 cm round glass or pottery dish of about 2 ins/5 cm in depth.
2. Put butter, syrup, treacle and sugar into a bowl. Leave uncovered and heat for 5 mins at defrost setting.
3. Stir in muesli then spread evenly into prepared dish. Leave uncovered and cook 4 mins at full power.
4. Stand 3 mins then cook a further 1 min at full power. Leave until quite cool then cut into 8 triangles with a sharp, round-topped knife.
5. Remove from dish when cold and store in an airtight container.

makes 8

DINNER PARTY MINTS

---

2 oz/50 g butter

---

2 tablespoons milk

---

1 teaspoon peppermint essence

---

1 lb/450 g icing sugar, sifted

---

green food colouring

---

makes about 1¼ lb/575 g

1. Put butter, milk and essence into a 3 pt/1.75 litre dish and heat 3 mins at defrost setting.
2. Work in icing sugar then add a few drops of green colouring, mixing until evenly tinted.
3. Knead until smooth then roll out to ½ inch/1.25 cm in thickness on a surface dusted with sifted icing sugar.
4. Cut into about 30 rounds with a 1 in/2.5 cm fluted cutter or 70 rounds with a ½ in/1.25 cm cutter. Leave 2 or 3 hours to dry out. If liked, brush one side of each with melted chocolate. Drop into paper sweet cases.

FRUIT AND NUT CUP CAKES

6 oz/175 g self-raising flour
pinch of salt
6 oz/175 g butter or margarine, at kitchen temperature
6 oz/175 g caster sugar
3 eggs (size 3) at kitchen temperature
1 oz/25 g sultanas or raisins
1 oz/25 g chopped walnuts or hazelnuts
3 tablespoons cold milk

makes 18 (F)

1. Sift flour and salt on to a plate. Put butter or margarine and sugar into a bowl and cream until very light and fluffy in consistency; also much paler than its original colour.
2. Beat in eggs, one at a time, adding 1 tablespoon sifted flour with each. Add fruit and nuts.
3. Lastly fold in rest of flour alternately with milk. When evenly combined, spoon mixture into 18 paper cases.
4. Stand, 6 at a time, on floor of oven in a ring. Allow plenty of space between each then bake 2–2½ mins at full power or until well risen.
5. Decorate when cold with a dusting of icing sugar and top with nuts or glacé cherries.

FRUIT BAPS

1 level teaspoon caster sugar
½ pt/275 ml water, with the chill off
1 level teaspoon dried yeast
1 lb/450 g plain strong brown flour
1 level teaspoon salt or salt substitute (the latter useful for those on low sodium diets)
1 oz/25 g butter or margarine

ADDITIONS
2 oz/50 g dried fruit

1 oz/25 g caster sugar

makes 16 (F)

1. Put sugar into a large cup or jug and mix with 6 tablespoons of water. Warm in the microwave for 1 min at defrost setting, leaving uncovered. Remove from oven.
2. Stir in yeast. Stand about 10 mins when yeast brew should foam up in the cup or jug and look like a glass of beer with a head.
3. Meanwhile sift flour and salt into a bowl. Warm in the microwave, uncovered, for 1 min at defrost setting.
4. Rub in butter or margarine finely then mix to a dough with yeast mixture and remaining water. Toss in the fruit and sugar.
5. Knead thoroughly until no longer sticky, and satiny-smooth, allowing about 10 mins.
6. Place in a lightly greased or oiled large bowl then cover bowl, not dough itself, with a piece of greased or oiled cling film. Puncture twice with the tip of a knife.
7. Warm in the microwave for 1 min at defrost setting. Rest 5 mins. Repeat 3 or 4 times until dough has doubled in size. Re-knead briefly.
8. Divide into 16 equal-sized pieces and shape into flattish rounds. Arrange round the edge of 2 large greased and floured dinner plates, putting 8 rounds on to each. Cover with kitchen paper and return to the microwave.
9. Warm 1 min at defrost setting then rest for 4 mins. Repeat 3 or 4 times or until Baps double in size. Sprinkle with brown flour and leave uncovered.
10. Cook each plate of rolls for 4 mins at full power, turning once unless oven has a turntable. Cool Baps on a wire rack.

CHOCOLATE NUT GÂTEAU

3 oz/75 g caster sugar

3 eggs (size 3) at kitchen temperature

3 oz/75 g plain flour, sifted twice for maximum aeration

FILLING
3½ oz/100 g plain chocolate

½ pt/275 ml double cream

2 tablespoons milk

hazelnuts or walnuts for decoration

serves 8 (F)

1. Line a 7 × 4 in/17.5 × 10 cm round glass dish smoothly with cling film. Make sure the dish is the same diameter top and bottom.
2. Tip sugar into a bowl and warm 2 mins at defrost setting. Add eggs and whisk steadily until mixture bulks up to almost 1 pt/575 ml and is as thick as whipped cream. It should also be very pale in colour.
3. Cut and fold in flour with a metal spoon, cutting side edge of spoon along base of bowl and flipping mixture over and over on itself until smoothly and evenly combined.
4. Spoon into prepared dish, leave uncovered and cook 4 mins at full power.
5. Remove from oven and leave to stand 10 mins before lifting out of dish (by holding edges of cling film) and transferring to a wire rack.
6. Peel film away when cake is completely cold. Cut sponge in half horizontally.
7. To make filling, put chocolate, broken into pieces, in a bowl. Cook 3–3½ mins at defrost setting to melt. Watch carefully as soon as it starts to melt. Leave until cool but still liquid.
8. Whip cream until thick. Gently whisk in melted chocolate alternately with milk. Sandwich cake together with just under half the Chocolate Cream. Pile remainder thickly over the top then stud with nuts. Chill lightly before serving.
Eat the same day; fatless sponges go stale quickly.

NOTE *Cake rises up to the top of the dish during the initial stages of cooking and falls to a depth of 2–3 in/5–7.5 cm. This is quite in order.*

COFFEE APRICOT GÂTEAU

A showpiece for special occasions, this luscious gâteau can be made in next to no time and is much less complicated to put together than it looks. To freeze, keep unwrapped and leave overnight until hard. Afterwards wrap carefully and place in a box. Unwrap before defrosting to prevent spoiling the coating.

4 digestive biscuits, finely crushed

8 oz/225 g butter or block margarine, at kitchen temperature and soft

8 oz/225 g dark brown soft sugar

4 eggs (size 3) at kitchen temperature

8 oz/225 g self-raising flour

3 tablespoons coffee and chicory essence

FILLING AND TOPPING
1 can (15 oz/425 g) apricot halves

½ pt/275 ml double cream

2 tablespoons coffee and chicory essence

3 oz/75 g flaked and toasted almonds

serves 8 (F)

1. Have ready 2 round glass or pottery buttered dishes, each 8–8½ in/20–21.5 cm in diameter by 1–1½ in/2.5–3.75 cm in depth. Dust base and sides with crushed biscuits.
2. Cream butter or margarine and sugar together until light and fluffy. Beat in eggs singly, adding a tablespoon of flour with each. Fold in rest of flour alternately with coffee and chicory essence.
3. When smooth and evenly combined, divide evenly between the 2 dishes. Leave uncovered. Bake individually, allowing 5 mins at full power and turning each 3 times unless one has a turntable.
4. Leave in dishes until lukewarm then carefully turn out and cool on a wire rack.
5. To complete, drain apricots (keep syrup for drinks, etc.) and coarsely chop up 2 of the halves. Whip cream until thick. Fold in coffee and chicory essence.
6. Take out a quarter of the cream and gently stir in chopped apricots. Use to sandwich both layers of cake together. Transfer to a serving plate.
7. Spread rest of cream over top and sides of cake then decorate top with apricots. Press almonds against sides then refrigerate about 1 hour before serving.

BLACK FOREST CHERRY ROULADE

Grand, stylish and heaven to eat is the only way I can describe this very rich and sumptuous roll. For me, personally, it works better in the microwave than it does when baked coventionally and is a marvellous centrepiece at dinner parties or luncheons. It does need a large capacity oven.

5 eggs (size 2)
$\frac{1}{8}$ teaspoon lemon juice
5 oz/150 g caster sugar
2 oz/150 g cocoa powder + $\frac{1}{2}$ oz/15 g cornflour sifted together twice onto a plate
1 tablespoon boiling water
icing sugar

FILLING
$\frac{1}{2}$ pt/275 ml double cream
1 tablespoon Kirsch or cherry brandy
1 large crushed milk flake bar
2 heaped tablespoons canned cherry pie filling

cuts into 10 slices

1. Lightly grease a 12 in/30 cm square plastic tray with shallow sides. Line with non-stick parchment paper, allowing it to protrude 1 in/2$\frac{1}{2}$ cm above top edge of tray all the way round to support mixture as it rises.
2. Separate eggs, putting whites into one bowl and yolks into another. Beat whites to a stiff snow with the lemon juice, using electric beaters for speed.
3. Add sugar to yolks and beat until very thick and pale in colour. Stir in cocoa and cornflour mixture, thinning down with the boiling water.
4. When smooth and evenly combined, gently beat in one-third of the egg whites. Finally fold in remaining whites with a large metal spoon or spatula, cutting smartly across base of bowl then flipping mixture over and over on itself.
5. Spread evenly to prepared tray and cook, uncovered, 7$\frac{1}{2}$–8 mins at full power, turning once. Remove from oven and inspect. If cake is very tacky along the edges, cook a further $\frac{1}{2}$–1 min.
6. Take out of oven and leave, in the tray, until completely cold. Turn out on to a piece of greaseproof paper or foil *thickly* dusted with sifted icing sugar. Carefully and gently peel away lining paper.

7. To complete, whip cream until thick then stir in remaining ingredients. Re-whip *briefly* then spread over Roulade. Roll up with the help of the paper on which it is standing.
8. The Roulade will crack but this is quite in order. Dredge thickly with more sifted icing sugar then, using two fish slices or large spatulas, transfer to a dish. Serve cut in slices.

GINGER AND ORANGE CAKE

The sort of cut-and-come-again cake that is close to the heart of all families. It cooks in an amazing 7 mins and keeps perfectly in an airtight container.

8 oz/225 g self-raising flour
pinch of salt
1$\frac{1}{2}$ level teaspoons mixed spice
4 oz/125 g butter or margarine, at kitchen temperature
4 oz/125 g light brown soft sugar
4 oz/125 g chopped, preserved ginger
2 level teaspoons finely grated orange peel
2 eggs (size 3) beaten with 5 tablespoons cold milk
icing sugar

serves 8 (F)

1. Sift flour, salt and spice into a bowl. Rub in butter or margarine finely. Toss in sugar, ginger and orange peel.
2. Add eggs and milk in one go, then stir to a soft consistency with a fork.
3. Spread evenly into an 8 in/20 cm round glass dish (deep and straight-sided), closely lined with cling film. Leave uncovered.
4. Cook 6$\frac{1}{2}$–7 mins at full power when cake should be well-risen and beginning to pull away from sides.
5. Remove from microwave and leave to stand $\frac{1}{4}$ hour. Lift out on to a wire cooling rack and carefully peel away film.
6. When completely cold, dust top with sifted icing sugar.

MOON DUST CAKE

American inspired, this is a dark-as-night chocolate cake with the texture of velvet and flavour of heaven. Best whizzed in a food processor, you can have the whole thing made and cooked in well under 30 mins.

3½ oz/100 g plain chocolate, at kitchen temperature
1 oz/25 g cocoa powder
8 oz/225 g plain flour
1 level teasooon bicarbonate of soda
5 oz/150 g butter, at kitchen temperature
7 oz/200 g light brown soft sugar
2 eggs (size 2)
½ teaspoon vanilla essence
¼ pt/150 ml buttermilk
3 tablespoons cold milk

FILLING
¼ pt/150 ml double cream
2 oz/50 g grated milk chocolate
1 level tablespoon caster sugar
1 level teaspoon grated lemon peel

serves 8 generously (F)

1. Line a 7 × 3½ in/17 × 9 cm soufflé-type dish with cling film, making sure it lies smoothly over base and sides.
2. Break up chocolate and put into a glass or pottery dish. Leave uncovered and melt 3–3½ mins at defrost setting. When ready, the chocolate will remain in its original shaped pieces but should be soft when touched. Remove from microwave and scrape into food processor bowl.
3. Add all remaining ingredients and blend until smooth. Stop machine, wipe down side of bowl with spatula and continue to run machine for a further ½ min.
4. Transfer to prepared dish, leave uncovered and cook 8 mins at full power, turning dish 4 times unless oven has a turntable.
5. Remove from oven. Cool to lukewarm in the dish (the cake drops to 2½ in/6.25 cm in depth and shrinks away from the sides but this is quite in order) then carefully lift out on to a wire cooling rack. Peel back film and leave until completely cold. Halve horizontally.
6. Whip the cream until thick, then stir in chocolate, sugar and lemon peel. Sandwich cake together with cream then swirl remainder thickly over the top. Chill lightly in the refrigerator before serving.

FRUITED MALT LOAF

At its best when served sliced and buttered

1 level teaspoon caster sugar
¼ pt/150 ml water, with the chill off
2 level teaspoon dried yeast
1 lb/450 g plain strong flour
½ level teaspoon salt
3 oz/75 g mixture of sultanas and raisins
4 level tablespoons malt
1 level tablespoon black treacle
1 oz/25 g butter or margarine
2–3 tablespoons skimmed milk

makes 2 (F)

1. Put sugar into a large cup or jug and mix with the water and dried yeast. Warm in the microwave for 1 min at defrost setting, leaving uncovered. Remove from oven.
2. Leave to stand about 10 mins when yeast brew should foam up in the cup or jug and look like a glass of beer with a head.
3. Meanwhile, sift flour and salt into a bowl then toss in the dried fruits.
4. Put malt, treacle and butter or margarine into a small basin, leave uncovered and melt 3 mins at defrost setting.
5. Add to flour with yeast liquid and sufficient milk to make a soft dough. Knead thoroughly for 10 mins then divide into 2 equal-sized pieces.
6. Shape to fit two ½ pt/850 ml oblong glass or pottery dishes, first well-greased. Cover dishes, not dough, with greased or oiled cling film. Puncture twice with the tip of a knife.
7. Warm in the microwave for 1 min at defrost setting then rest 5 mins. Repeat 3 or 4 times more or until loaves have doubled in size. Remove film.
8. Place side by side in the oven. Leave uncovered and cook 2 mins at full power. Reverse position of dishes and cook a further 2 mins. Repeat once more. Leave to stand 10 mins then turn loaves out on to a wire cooling rack.

WINE-SPICED PEACHES WITH GINGERBREAD

Serve with wedges of gingerbread, made in the microwave the day before

GINGERBREAD
6 oz/175 g plain flour
2 rounded teaspoons ground ginger
1 level teaspoon mixed spice
½ level teaspoon bicarbonate of soda
4 oz/125 g golden syrup
1 oz/25 g black treacle
1 oz/25 g dark brown soft sugar
1½ oz/40 g lard or white cooking fat
1 egg (size 1 or 2) well-beaten
4 tablespoons cold milk
8 large peaches
lemon juice
½ pt/275 ml dry red wine
6 oz/175 g caster sugar
2 in/5 cm piece of cinnamon stick
4 cloves
2 medium oranges, peeled and thinly sliced

serves 6–8

1. To make the gingerbread: have ready an oblong pie dish with rim, the inside measuring about 7½ × 5 × 2¼ in/ 19 × 12.5 × about 6 cm. Line base and sides smoothly with cling film. Alternatively, use a 6 in/15 cm glass or pottery soufflé-type dish.
2. Sift flour, ginger, spice and bicarbonate of soda into a fairly large mixing bowl.
3. Put syrup, treacle, brown sugar and lard or cooking fat into a separate bowl. Heat 2–3 mins at full power or until fat has just melted. Do not cover.
4. Remove from oven and stir well to blend. Add to dry ingredients with egg and milk.
5. Mix to a fairly soft consistency with a fork, stirring briskly without beating. Pour into dish and leave uncovered. Cook 3–4 mins at full power, turning dish 4 times unless oven has a turntable. When ready, Gingerbread should be well-risen with a hint of a shine across the top.

6. Leave to stand 10 mins inside or outside the oven, whichever is the most convenient. Lift out of dish and stand on a wire rack.
7. Peel away film from sides to allow steam to escape. Remove film from underneath when Gingerbread is cold. Store in an airtight container, and leave 1 day before cutting.
8. Puncture skin of peaches by nicking once or twice with a knife. Put into a bowl and cover with water. Leave 2 mins. Drain and cover with cold water. Drain again and remove skins.
9. Cut each peach in half and twist to separate. Remove stones. Brush halves all over with lemon juice.
10. Put wine, sugar, cinnamon stick and cloves into an 8 × 2 in/20 × 5 cm round dish. Cover with an inverted plate and heat 4 mins at full power.
11. Stir round, add peaches (cut sides down) and baste with wine mixture. Decorate with slices of orange, placing them between the peaches. Cover with cling film, puncturing it twice with the tip of a knife. Alternatively, cover with matching lid.
12. Cook 10 mins at full power, turning dish 4 times unless oven has a turntable. Leave to cool then refrigerate until well-chilled before serving with the gingerbread.

JAFFA WINE MULL

2 large grapefruit
1 pt/575 ml medium dry red wine
2 in/5 cm piece of cinnamon stick
3 cloves
4 oz/125 g granulated sugar
2 tablespoons whisky or brandy

serves 5 to 6

1. Halve grapefruit and sqeeze out juice. Strain into a large bowl then add wine, cinnamon stick, cloves and sugar.
2. Cover with a plate and heat 6–8 mins at full power, stirring at least twice. Remove from oven and leave to stand 5 mins.
3. Stir round again and add whisky or brandy. Ladle into handled cups or glasses and serve.

INDEX